Scottish Studies: O-Grade Geography

Peter Gilchrist

Edward Arnold

© Peter Gilchrist 1984

**First published in Great Britain 1984
by Edward Arnold (Publishers) Ltd.,
41 Bedford Square
London WC1B 3DQ**

**Edward Arnold (Australia) Pty Ltd.,
80 Waverley Road, Caulfield East,
Victoria 3145, Australia**

Reprinted 1984 (twice), 1986

British Library Cataloguing in Publication Data

Gilchrist, Peter
    Scottish studies: 0-grade geography.
    1. Scotland — Description and travel — 1951
    I. Title
    914.11   DA867

ISBN 0-7131-0672-7

Note to teachers

The following is a list of Ordnance Survey
maps which are referred to throughout the
book. Pupils should be issued with the
relevant maps around which many exercises
are based. Each of the maps have been
assigned a number from 1 to 10 for ease of
reference.

Map No.	Extract Number	Date	Area
1	186M/60	1971	Dumbarton
2	197M/49	1971	Blairgowrie
3	220M/70	1971	Melrose
4	171M/67	1971	Cumnock
5	2nd Series Sheet 64	1980	E. Kilbride
6	2nd Series Sheet 65	1979	Forth Bridges
7	251M/26	1971	Torridon
8	2nd Series Sheet 33	1980	Skye
9	2nd Series 383/36	1976	Aviemore
10	2nd Series Sheet 21	1980	Cromarty Firth

Set in 11/12pt IBM Press Roman by 🅰 Tek-Art,
Croydon, Surrey
Printed in Great Britain by Thomson Litho Ltd.,
East Kilbride

Contents

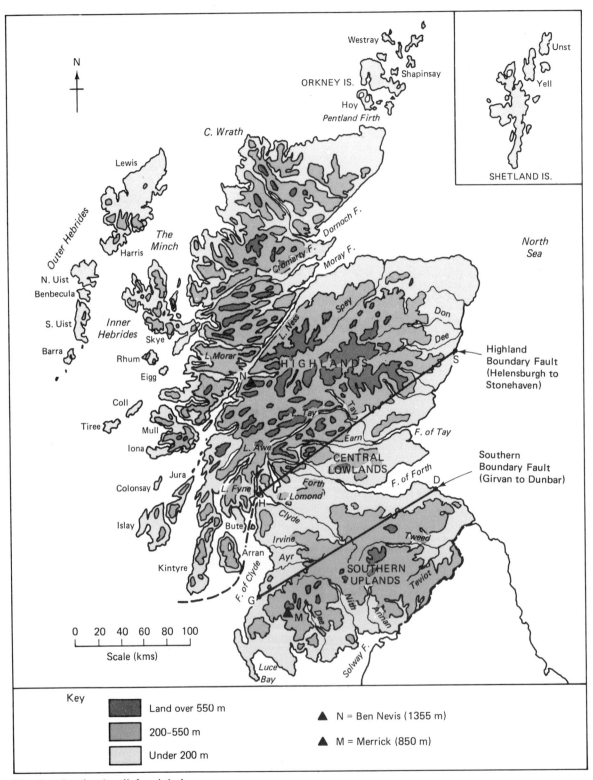

Fig. 1 Scotland: relief and drainage

1
Understanding Scotland through maps

Scotland forms one part of the United Kingdom, along with England, Wales and Northern Ireland. If you look at a map of the world, you will see that Scotland is very small compared with some of the other countries. Nevertheless, Scotland is a beautiful land, full of variety and interest and thousands of people from all over the world visit every year. But what is Scotland like to live in? We all know what it is like to live in our home town, but do people all over Scotland live similar lives and see the same everyday things as we do? The answer to this question is simply **no**. Despite its small size, Scotland is a land of many contrasting landscapes. We are going to look at a few of these landscapes and try to explain how different factors have influenced them and find out what life is like within each.

Scotland's three physical sections

A study of Fig. 1 shows evidence of the variety of landscapes. Scotland can be divided into three main physical sections:

1 The Highlands

This is the most northerly section. It is an area made up mainly of high hills and exposed steep slopes where the only low, flat land lies around the coast or in deep valleys (see Fig. 2).

2 The Southern Uplands

This is the most southerly section. It is also a hilly area but the hills are lower and slopes less steep and exposed than those of the Highlands.

Fig. 2   A highland landscape

3 The Central Lowlands

This, as the name suggests, is an area of much lower land lying between the Highlands and Southern Uplands. Although there are hills in this area they are fewer in number and much lower.

Before studying the geography of Scotland in detail, you should study Fig. 1 carefully until you are familiar with Scotland's three sections, its main rivers, islands and estuaries.

The building up of Scotland's landscape

Natural landscapes all over the world have been formed as a result of many different processes, working over millions of years. This of course applies to the landscape of Scotland.

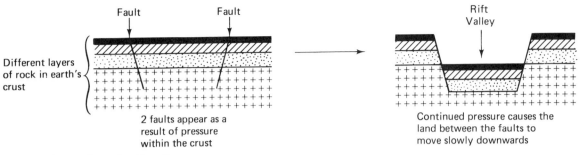

Different layers of rock in earth's crust

Fault   Fault

2 faults appear as a result of pressure within the crust

Rift Valley

Continued pressure causes the land between the faults to move slowly downwards

Fig. 3   Formation of a rift valley

The oldest rocks in Scotland were laid down as sediments over 500 million years ago, beneath an ancient sea. Because of incredible pressure caused by movements within the earth's crust, they were then crushed to form solid rock, raised above sea level and folded to form an upland plateau. Such pressure also caused many of the old rocks to crack and great **faults** were formed running from **south-west** to **north-east** across the land. One of these faults (now called the Highland Boundary Fault) extended from the position of Helensburgh north-eastwards to the position of Stonehaven, while another, the Southern Boundary Fault, extended from the position of Girvan to that of Dunbar (see Fig. 1). Since then the land between these faults has been forced downwards forming the **rift valley** which we now know as the Central Lowlands (see Fig. 3).

Folding and faulting were not the only movements within the earth's crust to affect Scotland's landscape. With all this folding and faulting taking place the crust was weakened at several points and as a result molten magma from the **mantle** forced its way into the crust (pushing the sediments above up with it) and then cooled down beneath the surface to form the great granite hills found in the Highlands and Southern Uplands today. Continued pressure combined with the heat from the molten magma also caused many of the older rocks to change completely into new extremely hard rocks. In other areas the magma forced its way right onto the earth's surface, forming volcanic hills. This is why the Central Lowlands has several areas of hills today (see Fig. 4).

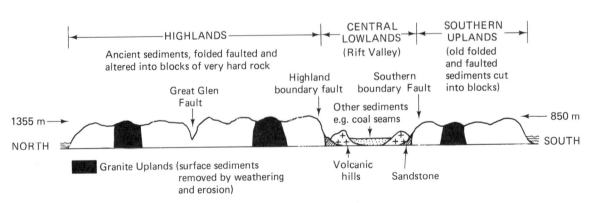

HIGHLANDS

Ancient sediments, folded faulted and altered into blocks of very hard rock

CENTRAL LOWLANDS
(Rift Valley)

SOUTHERN UPLANDS
(old folded and faulted sediments cut into blocks)

Great Glen Fault

Highland boundary fault

Southern boundary Fault

Other sediments e.g. coal seams

1355 m →

NORTH

← 850 m

SOUTH

Granite Uplands (surface sediments removed by weathering and erosion)

Volcanic hills

Sandstone

Fig. 4   A side-view or cross-section of Scotland from north to south

The wearing away of Scotland's landscape

No sooner had such uplands been formed, however, than the processes of weathering and erosion began to wear them down again. Pieces of rock were broken off from the uplands and deposited in surrounding lakes and seas e.g. in the area now known as the Central Lowlands. The type of rock laid down depended greatly on the climate existing at the time. It is important to remember that Scotland's climate has not always been the same as it is today; it has changed several times over millions of years. For example, the sandstone found in many parts of the Central Lowlands was deposited when the climate was very much drier, while the coal-bearing rocks were formed when our climate was much more like that of the lands around the equator today, i.e. hot and wet. The climate continued to change and Scotland experienced an 'Ice Age' with conditions similar to those found in arctic regions today. When temperatures were at their lowest, great ice sheets moved slowly over Scotland, lowering and rounding the tops of the mountains, while during times of less severe temperatures rivers of ice, called **glaciers** (see Fig. 5), made their way along fault lines where the rocks were weakest. They carved out valleys of their own and deposited the eroded material **(moraine)** when they reached the lowlands or surrounding seas. This made slopes in the uplands much steeper because the valleys carved by the glaciers were

Fig. 5   A glacier

extremely deep — glaciers are much more powerful agents of erosion than rivers.

Since the last Ice Age the climate has changed again and become warmer although it is still wet. As a result, the main agents of erosion are the sea (which continually wears away some parts of our coastline and deposits material on other parts) and rivers which are wearing away Scotland's uplands, depositing loads further down forming new areas of coastal plain. Weathering, e.g. by frost action, heating and cooling and the dissolving of rock by acid rainwater, still helps the processes of erosion and deposition to form new landscapes. Our landscape never stops changing — it is being altered now as you read this book.

Exercise

1 Copy and complete the following paragraph, using your atlas and the information given in this chapter to help you. All the answers are provided below the paragraph (p. 8) but they are not in the correct order.

Scotland lies between latitudes _____ and _____ and longitudes _____ and _____. Although at one time it was a kingdom on its own, today it forms one region of the United Kingdom, along with England, _____ and _____ _____ . Scotland lies off the north-west coast of the continent of _____, between the _____ Sea to the east and the _____ Ocean to the west.

The western coast is indented with many inlets and dotted with many islands. Among the largest of these are L _____ S _____ and M _____.

The eastern coast has a much smoother appearance, although there are three major firths or estuaries cutting into it. These are called the Firth of F _____, the Firth of T _____ and the M _____ Firth.

Two large groups of islands lie to the north-east of Scotland: the _____ Islands and the _____ Islands. The mainland consists of three major physical sections: 1. the H _____, consisting mainly of high uplands rising to _____ metres at the summit of B _____ N _____; 2. the S _____ U _____, an area consisting largely of lower hills rising to _____ metres at the summit of _____ (in both these areas lowland is restricted to river valleys and coastal plains); 3. the C _____ L _____, an area of much flatter land where hills are fewer and lower than those of the two upland areas.

Each region is drained by many rivers, the longer ones flowing mainly towards the _____ e.g. the River Tw_____, River T _____ and River S_____. One very long river (perhaps Scotland's most famous) flows northwards from the Southern Uplands, through the Central Lowlands into its own Firth. This river is the River _____.

North   Forth   Tay   54° north   Northern Ireland
Lewis   61° north   Mull   Clyde   850   Southern
Uplands   Central Lowlands   Tweed   east   Spey
0°   Atlantic   Skye   Moray   1355   9° west
Wales   Europe   Orkney   Highlands   Ben Nevis
Merrick   Tay   Shetland

2 Look carefully at Fig. 4 then answer the following questions.

(a) The diagram shows that much of the upland of Scotland consists of ancient sediments laid down beneath an ancient sea millions of years ago. Explain in your own words how they then became uplands.

(b) Many of the highest mountains in Scotland are shown to be made of granite.

(i) What does this suggest about the hardness of granite?
(ii) Explain your answer.
(iii) Explain how these granite uplands were formed.
(iv) Granite was formed **beneath** the earth's surface, and yet today it reaches the surface of many hills. Explain why.

(c) 'In Scotland's Uplands the hills are separated by extremely deep, steep-sided valleys, much deeper and steeper than those which could have been formed by rivers.' Explain this statement.

(d) What is meant by a **fault**?

(e) Explain, using diagrams, why the Central Lowlands of Scotland lie at a much lower level than the Highlands and Southern Uplands.

(f) Explain why there are still areas of low hills in the Central Lowlands.

3 Explain the following statements giving examples where possible:

(a) 'The changes in climate over millions of years have had a great effect on the type of rock laid down in the Central Lowlands.'

(b) 'Scotland's landscape never stands still — it is continually changing.'

Where do people live in Scotland?

Exercise

Examine Fig. 6 carefully and compare it with Fig. 1, then copy and complete the following paragraph. The answers are found below but they are not in the correct order.

Fig. 6 shows that four of Scotland's largest settlements i.e. _____ , _____ , _____ , _____ lie within the _____ _____ . The only city with over 80 000 people which lies outside this area is _____ . Furthermore the most densely populated areas of Scotland lie within a band stretching from the Firth of _____ in West Central Scotland to the Firth of _____ in the east. The only areas where few people live in Central Scotland are the areas of low _____ . In the Highlands and Southern Uplands most settlement is restricted to _____ _____ and _____ _____ . In the Highlands most people live on a broad plain along the _____ coast, while settlement along the _____ coast is limited to a very narrow band. In the Southern Uplands the most densely populated areas are found in the valley of the River _____ in the east and along the coast of the _____ Firth in the south.

Edinburgh   Aberdeen   Forth   hills   river valleys
Glasgow   Paisley   Clyde   east   west   Tweed
Dundee   Central Lowlands   coastal plains   Solway

Note: this paragraph only describes Scotland's population distribution, it does not explain it. A look at Scotland's geography in more detail is necessary and so we shall refer to Ordnance Survey maps to help us.

Ordnance Survey mapwork

Ordnance Survey symbols

Many features of the landscape are represented by simple symbols on Ordnance Survey (O.S.) maps. These symbols are shown in Fig. 7 and it is important to become familiar with them.

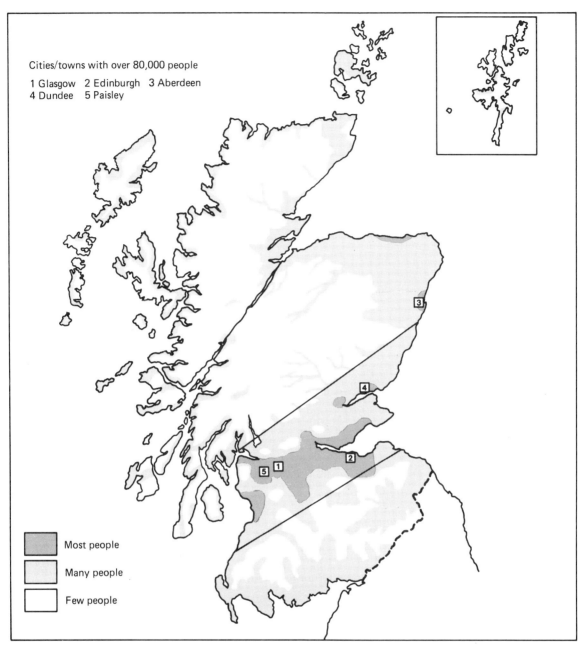

Cities/towns with over 80,000 people

1 Glasgow   2 Edinburgh   3 Aberdeen
4 Dundee   5 Paisley

Most people

Many people

Few people

Fig. 6   Population distribution in Scotland

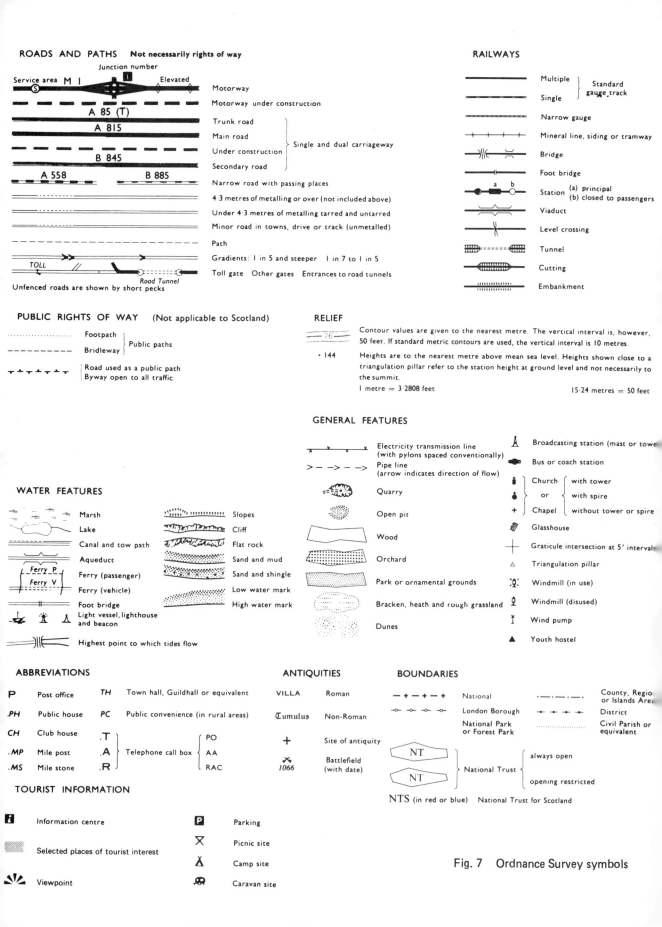

Fig. 7 Ordnance Survey symbols

Distance

The real distance between two points on a map can be found by using the map's **scale** (the scale is the number of times greater the distance is in real life than the distance on the map). The scale is usually shown at the bottom of Ordnance Survey maps in three ways i.e.
1. By a **ratio** e.g., 1:50 000 (1 cm on the map represents 50 000 cm or ½ kilometre in real life).
2. By a **statement** e.g., 2 centimetres to 1 kilometre (2 cm on the map represents 1 km in real life).
3. By a **scale line**. Look at Fig. 8.

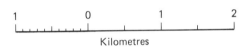

Fig. 8

In order to calculate the real distance between two points A and B, the simplest method is as follows: –
1. Place an edge of a piece of paper on the map so that both points A and B lie on the edge, then mark the two points on the paper (Fig. 9a).

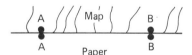

Fig. 9 a)

2. Take the edge of your paper down to the scale line, place point A at 0 km and read off the distance at point B. In Fig. 9b, points A and B are 1½ km (1500 metres) apart.
Note: if the distance between A and B is longer than the scale line, it is necessary to mark off each kilometre on the paper and continually move the paper back to 0 km.

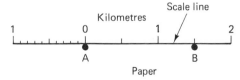

Fig. 9 b)

Exercise

1 Copy the symbols in Fig.7.

2 Use the scale line in Fig. 8 to calculate the distances in Fig. 10:

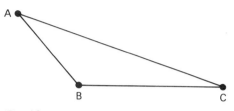

Fig. 10

(a) from point A to point B;
(b) from point B to point C;
(c) from point A to point C.

Grid references

Every Ordnance Survey map is covered by a grid of small squares. On the 1:50 000 maps (used in this book) each square is 2 cm long and represents 1 square kilometre on the ground. This 'National Grid' of squares can be used to find any place on a map. In order to make this job easier each square is given a 'name'.

Naming a square – four-figure grid references
Each square is given a **name** or **grid reference** using the numbers found on each side of the map. Numbers running west to east along the top and bottom of a map are called **eastings**, while those running from south to north are called **northings**. Each square is named by first taking the easting bounding the square on its left side and then taking the northing bounding the square on its bottom side. For example the easting in the shaded square in Fig. 11 is 28 and the northing is 06. Therefore the grid reference or name of the shaded square is 2806.

Naming a point – six-figure grid references
To be more accurate about the position of any point six-figure grid references are used. Imagine the shaded square in Fig. 11 is divided into **tenths** along its easting and

11

northing i.e. that the square is divided into 100 smaller squares. Point X would be roughly 7 of these smaller squares along from easting 28 and 2 smaller squares up from northing 06. The six-figure grid reference of point X would therefore be 287062.

Exercise

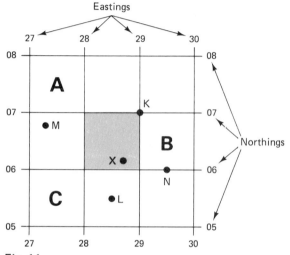

Fig. 11

Examine Fig. 11:—
(a) Give the four-figure grid references for squares A, B and C.
(b) Give the six-figure grid references for points K, L, M and N.

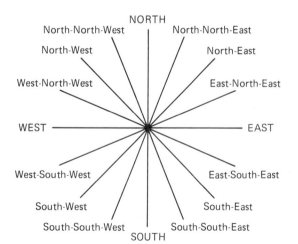

Fig. 12

Direction

When describing direction we shall assume that North means directly towards the top of a map i.e. we shall use **grid north**. All the directions on the 16 point compass can be seen in Fig. 12. In Fig. 11, if we travelled from point X to point M we would be travelling in a west-north-westerly direction.

Exercise

Examine O.S. Map 1
1 Write down the scale of the map in 3 different ways.

2 Which features can be found at the following grid-references:—
  (a) 497 709
  (b) 492 697
  (c) 397 754
  (d) 366 762
  (e) 532 722
  (f) 499 696
  (g) 450 753 to 460 756
  (h) 355 757

3 Examine the railway along the **south** bank of the estuary (the Firth of Clyde), through Langbank and Bishopton.
  (a) Railways tend to avoid steep slopes, why is this? Write down three ways in which builders have been able to keep this railway line running fairly level (the following grid references may help you 441 698, 439 702, 428 722).
  (b) In which compass direction would you be travelling from point 437 705 to 446 690?
  (c) Is there any map evidence of Roman occupation in this area? Name at least three pieces of evidence giving six-figure grid references.

4 Using Fig. 11, in which of the 16 compass directions would you be travelling from:
  (a) point K to point L;
  (b) point X to point N;
  (c) point M to point L;
  (d) point N to point M;
  (e) point N to point X?

Drawing a sideview or cross-section

An examination of Ordnance Survey maps, shows that much of the land is covered with thin brown lines, these are called **contours**.

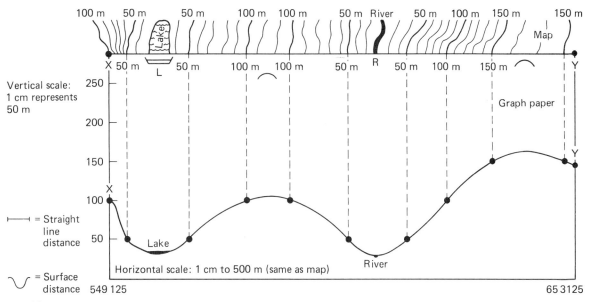

Fig. 13

They join points of equal height above sea level and therefore enable us to have a mental picture of what the landscape looks like i.e. how steep or gentle it is. The steeper the land the **closer** the lines. On newer O.S. maps contours indicate a difference in height or **a vertical interval** of 10 metres and on older maps approximately 15 metres.

In order to accurately understand what a landscape looks like side views or **cross-sections** of the landscape can be drawn. Fig. 13 shows a cross-section drawn between two points X and Y. Study Fig. 13 and read the following instructions on how to draw a cross-section.

1. Lay the top edge of a piece of graph paper along the section X to Y on the map.
2. Mark in pencil the crossing point of contours and water features on the edge of the graph paper.
3. Label each mark with its height and indicate water features, hills and valleys in pencil e.g.
R = river   ⌒ = hills   ∪ = valleys
    ⊂⇁ = lakes
4. Note the **highest** point, and choose and mark on a suitable **vertical scale** e.g., 1 cm to 50 metres.
5. Draw a horizontal base-line equal to the

length of the section, and add the **grid references** of X and Y. Then add a horizontal scale (which is equal to the scale of the map).
6. Drop vertical guide-lines in pencil from the marks at the edge of the paper to the appropriate height on the section.
7. Join all the points at the bottom of the guide-lines with a smooth curve, and add the relevant features.
8. Rub out all pencil lines and markings.
Note: if the contours are fairly close together on the map, it is not necessary to mark **every** one onto the graph paper. In Fig. 13 the darker contours were used to form an accurate cross-section from X to Y.

Exercise

Examine each of the contour diagrams (Fig. 14a, b, c and d) and draw a cross-section of each from A to B to reveal the landscape feature shown. Label the completed cross-sections, with one of the following terms:—
Hill, Steep slope, Valley, Gentle slope.

Calculating gradients

The **gradient** indicates how **steep** a slope is

13

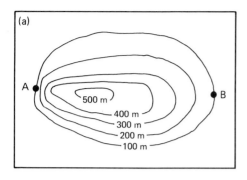

(a)

500 m
400 m
300 m
200 m
100 m

A   B

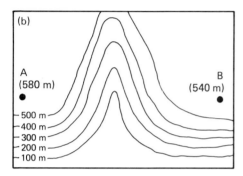

(b)

A (580 m)   B (540 m)

500 m
400 m
300 m
200 m
100 m

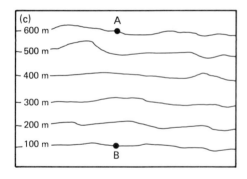

(c)

A

600 m
500 m
400 m
300 m
200 m
100 m

B

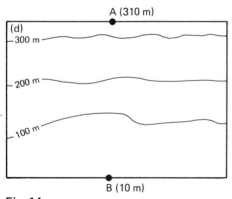

A (310 m)

(d)

300 m
200 m
100 m

B (10 m)

Fig. 14

between two points. The following formula is used to calculate the gradient between two points.

$$\text{Gradient} = \frac{\text{Difference in height}}{\text{Horizontal distance}}$$

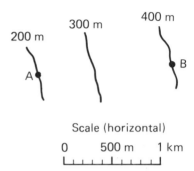

200 m   300 m   400 m

A   B

Scale (horizontal)

0   500 m   1 km

Look at the contours above. Point A is 200 metres above sea level and at a distance of 1400 metres from point B which is 400 metres above sea level. Using the formula the gradient would be:—

$$\frac{400 - 200}{1400} = \frac{200}{1400} = \frac{1}{7}$$

The answer is **1 in 7**, which means for every 7 metres along the ground the land rises by 1 metre (so a 1 in 7 slope is steeper than a 1 in 10 but not as steep as a 1 in 4). The answer is always expressed as 1 in X.

Calculating the range of altitude

The **range** is the difference in altitude between two points. Using the above example the highest point = 400 metres, the lowest point = 200 metres, the range = 200 metres.

Exercise

O.S. Map 1
1 Examine the map carefully and draw a cross-section of the landscape from Overtoun Muir (287 m) at 371 799 to the junction of the A class and minor road at 376 759. Mark on the following features: Overtoun Muir (287 m), Fort, Minor Road (yellow on map), Farm Track, Small Wood, 'A' Class Road.

2 Imagine you walked from point 377 789 on the minor road mentioned above to the top of Overtoun Muir.

    (a) In which of the 16 compass directions would you be walking?

    (b) Using your map how far (horizontally) would you have walked?

    (c) Through what **range** in altitude would you have walked?

    (d) What would the average **gradient** of this slope be i.e. how steep is it?

Relief and drainage

The **relief** is the height, shape and slope of the land. The **drainage** is the amount and shape of the water features on or below the earth's surface.

    When describing the **relief** of an area it is important to consider the following:

1. Its general height,
2. The highest and lowest points,
3. The names and shapes of the main hills e.g. are they rounded or rugged?
4. The names of any valleys, the direction in which they run and whether they are straight or winding.
5. The steepness of the main slopes (if a single slope in which direction does it run?),
6. Evidence of glaciation,
7. Any other physical features e.g. cliffs, caves, peninsulas.

Drainage

When describing the **drainage** of an area these features should be referred to:

1. The number of rivers, lakes or any other water features shown,
2. The names of the main water features,
3. Whether the rivers are winding or straight,
4. The direction in which they flow,
5. Whether they are fast or slow flowing,
6. Whether they are artificial (unnatural), few natural features are perfectly straight,
7. Whether there are any marshes i.e. are any areas poorly drained?

Note: Descriptions of specific features such as relief and drainage do not include information about farms, roads, etc., these are irrelevant in these cases.

Exercise

O.S. Map 2

1 Describe the relief and drainage of the following squares:
2650, 2342, 1636.

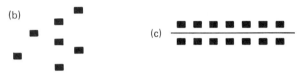

Fig. 15

Settlement patterns — refer to O.S. Map 3

A **settlement** is any building or group of buildings which is (or has been) inhabited by people e.g. farm or town, and is represented by grey buildings on older maps and pink buildings on newer maps.

    Settlements vary in shape and size and are affected by factors such as relief, drainage, industry, communications, etc. The three most common shapes or patterns are:

(a) Nucleated (buildings packed into a tight group) (Fig. 15a),
(b) Dispersed (buildings scattered) (Fig. 15b),
(c) Linear (buildings in a line) or ribbon-like (Fig. 15c).

    When estimating the size of settlements it is important to remember three things:

1. Each grid square has an area of 1 km² (1 square kilometre),
2. If the settlement is so small that it lies completely within one square, simply estimate the proportion of the square it covers to the nearest tenth e.g. Stichill covers about $\frac{1}{5}$ ($\frac{2}{10}$) of the area of square 7138 therefore the area of Stichill is approximately 0.2 square

kilometres (0.2 km²),
3. If the settlement lies within more than one square you should estimate the area it covers in each square then add these areas together. For example Kelso (including Maxwellheugh) would cover an area of:
0.1 km² in square 7232
0.2 km² in square 7233
0.6 km² in square 7234
0.1 km² in square 7334
0.2 km² in square 7333
—————
1.2 km²

Total area of Kelso is approximately 1.2 km²

Land use

The land use is very simply the use to which an area of land is put, e.g. rough grazing, housing, forestry etc. It may, however, include areas which are **not** used by people e.g. marshland. The main land uses are indicated by symbols or names on the map. In some cases, however, it is not always obvious what the land is used for but usually there are clues on the map which suggest possible uses. It is important to consider the following:
1. Areas which are poor for farming include high exposed areas (which are too cold and windy for most types of farming), steep slopes (where soils are thin and machinery cannot be used), glaciated uplands (where soils are particularly thin), marshy areas (where soils are too damp for most farming) — such areas are usually used (if at all) for **rough grazing.**
2. Areas which are good for farming are usually flat or low-lying, are well drained (either by rivers or drainage ditches) with no marshes, and are sheltered by higher land or woodland.
3. The best land for building is again flat, low and well drained.
4. Small areas of woodland may be found around farmhouses or large estate houses to shield them against the wind and beautify the landscape, while long thin strips of woodland are usually used as 'wind-breaks' or 'shelter belts' which protect farmers' fields against the wind.

Exercise

O.S. Map 4
1 (a) Draw a **cross-section** of the landscape from point A (the 575 m spot height) at grid reference 647 104 to point B (Craigdullyeart Hill) at grid reference 659 159. *3 marks*
(b) What general feature does this cross-section reveal? *½ mark*
(c) Mark on the following landscape features: trunk road, minor road, River Nith, railway, Meikle Westland Farm, and two woodland areas. *3½ marks*
(d) Trains cannot travel up steep gradients. How has the railway avoided steep slopes, while still remaining straight? Name 2 ways in which this is achieved. *2 marks*
(e) If you walked from point A to point B in which direction would you be going? *1 mark*

2 (a) What is the range of altitude from point 598 272 to the top of Auchenlongford Hill at 595 296. *1 mark*
(b) What is the **gradient** of this slope? *1 mark*
(c) The area enclosed by the square shown in Fig. 16 is a poor agricultural area. Using at least three pieces of evidence from the map explain why. *1½ marks*

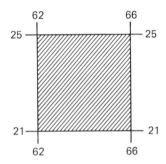

Fig. 16

O.S. Map 3
3 Copy and complete Fig. 17. Choose your answers from — **nucleated, dispersed** and **linear.** *1½ marks*

4 Estimate the size of Earlston (5738) and Smailholm (6436) in square kilometres. *1 mark*

SETTLEMENT	Grid reference	Settlement pattern
HEITON	714306	
STICHILL	714383	
Buildings around CHARLESFIELD	square 5829	

Fig. 17

5 Describe and explain the **land use** in the following squares:
5432, 6728, 7029, 7233. *4 marks*

6 Match each of the three grid references 555 328, 603 354 and 728 351 with one of the following descriptions:
    (a) This is a church lying about 62 m above sea level,
    (b) This steep-sided hill was used by early man,
    (c) This farm is approximately 183 m above sea level,
    (d) This is a clubhouse for golfers,
    (e) This is an orchard on the north slope of a valley. *3 marks*

7 In Fig. 18 there are three drainage features labelled A, B and C. Choose the appropriate description from the following list for each letter:
River Tweed, drainage ditch, marsh, waterfall, lake.
3 marks

8 Why is it unlikely that feature C is a natural feature?
1 mark

9 Although there is a small woodland area in square 5436 much of the land in the square is only fit for one type of farming. Using map evidence state what type of farming this is and, by describing the **relief** and **drainage** of the square, explain why this square is not suitable for other types of farming. *3 marks*

Total 30 marks

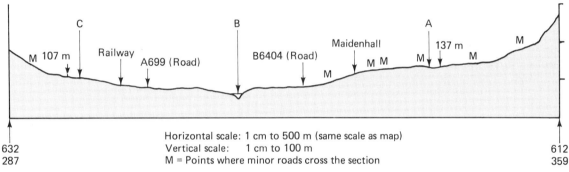

Horizontal scale: 1 cm to 500 m (same scale as map)
Vertical scale:　1 cm to 100 m
M = Points where minor roads cross the section

632
287

612
359

Fig. 18

2
Farming

A farm has often been described as an 'open air factory' where the farmer must make important decisions in an attempt to make a **profit**. Seeds, labour, fertilizer and machinery have to be paid for in the coming year and the farmers standard of living has to be maintained.

Like a factory manager the farmer must use several **inputs** in an attempt to produce **outputs** which will make a profit. Some of these inputs cost nothing while others can cost a great deal.

Exercise

1 Copy Fig. 19 and complete it by filling in the following words under the correct heading:
soil   flowers   fruit   rain   warmth   sunlight
vegetables   seeds   fertilizers   machinery

labour   milk   wool   young animals   older (larger) animals.

2 Colour the diagram as follows:
outputs = red, inputs which cost nothing = green, inputs which cost money = yellow.

Factors affecting the farmer

In Fig. 19 it appears that the farm operates under ideal conditions and that the farmer can grow anything he wishes. This is seldom the case. No two farms are in exactly the same location or are affected by exactly the same factors, each one has advantages and disadvantages. What the farmer must do is decide how best to use the land available in order to make a profit. This decision is influenced by two main groups of factors (see Fig. 20):

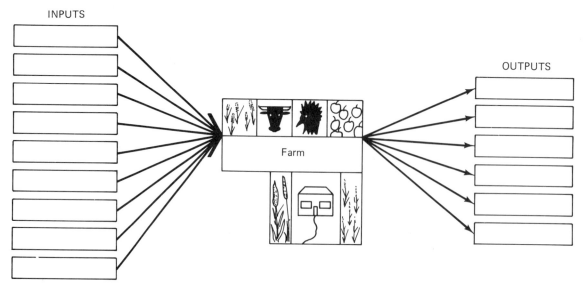

Fig. 19   The farm. Its inputs and outputs

Rain

Temperature

Soil

Slope

I want to make a profit. What shall I produce?

What do these factors allow you to produce?

What do these factors encourage you to produce?

LTD.(GROCER)

Market

Government policy

Farmer's assets

Sheep?   Cattle?   Fruit?   Cereals?

Fig. 20   Factors influencing the farmer

A. Physical factors

The basis of all farmers' wealth is the plants which grow on farms whether they are grown for their own value or for feeding animals. If any plant is to grow it must have a length of time during which its requirements of rainfall, sunlight and temperature are satisfied i.e. a growing season. This growing season varies throughout Scotland (see Fig. 21) due to four main factors:—

1. Rainfall (and sunshine) (see Fig. 22)
Due to Scotland's damp climate, there are few parts of the country where plants do not get enough moisture to grow. The opposite is in fact more often the case. As Fig. 23 indicates, most of Scotland's rainwater is blown in from

Scale (kms)

0   100

N

Over 37 weeks

34–37 weeks

31–34 weeks

Less than 31 weeks

Fig. 21   Average length of growing season

19

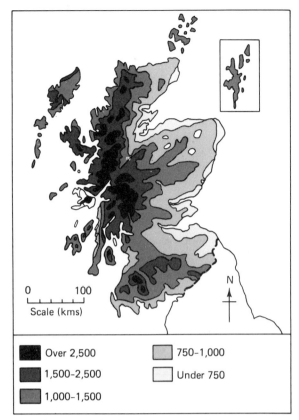

Fig. 22   Precipitation (mm per year)

Legend:
- Over 2,500
- 1,500–2,500
- 1,000–1,500
- 750–1,000
- Under 750

Scale (kms)
0   100

Fig. 24   Dairy Cattle

In the west the wetter climate encourages the growth of **permanent grass** and so **dairy cattle** (Fig. 24), which need large amounts of succulent grass, can be reared to produce milk in the lower parts of South West Scotland. This high rainfall does however lead to **acidity** in the soil and so many farmers must continually drain or add alkaline **lime** so that the grass or crops can grow well.

Unfortunately, in the Western Highlands the rainfall is so high that much of the acidic soil has turned to **peat** and, as a result of this and the other physical problems of the area, farming along the coast and valleys can only be carried out on a **part-time** basis by **crofters**.

In Eastern Scotland however, the drier, sunnier climate encourages **arable farming** where the fields are ploughed for the growing of crops like barley, wheat and oats either, for rearing and fattening livestock like sheep and beef cattle or, (in the best lowland soils) for sale (see Figs. 25 and 26).

the Atlantic by the prevailing south-westerly winds, and is dropped on the higher western slopes.

By the time the air reaches eastern areas, it has lost most of its moisture and so eastern Scotland is both **drier** and **sunnier** i.e. it lies in a **'rain shadow'** (remember that this not only applies to the Highlands, but to the Central Lowlands and Southern Uplands as well).

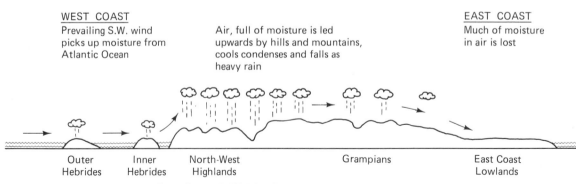

WEST COAST
Prevailing S.W. wind picks up moisture from Atlantic Ocean

Air, full of moisture is led upwards by hills and mountains, cools condenses and falls as heavy rain

EAST COAST
Much of moisture in air is lost

Outer Hebrides   Inner Hebrides   North-West Highlands   Grampians   East Coast Lowlands

Fig. 23   West-east transect of the Scottish Highlands

Fig. 25   Ploughing

Fig. 26   Beef cattle

2. Temperature

This is an important factor since most plants only start to grow when temperatures are above 6°C as frost kills many plants. The average temperature varies throughout Scotland due to four factors.

(a) Latitude. In general summer temperatures are lower in the north than in the south, but since Scotland covers only a small area the difference in temperature is very small (2–3°C) and so latitude has only a small effect on the growing season. In fact the longer summer days in the north often make up for the slight temperature difference.

(b) Altitude. This is much more important since temperatures drop 6°C for every 1000 m of altitude above sea level. As a result there is little or no cultivated land in Scotland above 300 m, so much of the Highlands and Southern Uplands are uncultivated.

(c) Aspect i.e. the direction in which a farm faces. Because Scotland is in the Northern Hemisphere, farms on slopes facing south tend to have more light and heat from the sun than those on north-facing slopes. Consider Fig. 27, which shows a valley running from east to west. It shows that the south-facing slope has sun shining directly on it while the north-facing slope has little direct light. As a result, in upland areas most farms tend to be

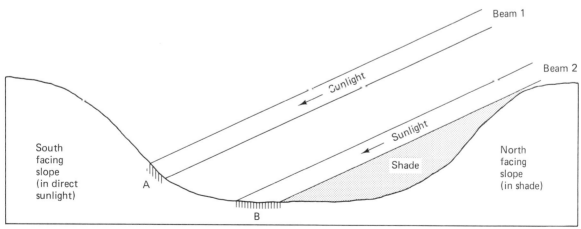

Fig. 27   Aspect

located on the south-facing slopes while the duller north-facing slopes tend to be forested.

Notice too that two equally powerful parallel beams from the sun are shining on the valley. Since Beam 1 falls on a smaller area on the valley side (area A) than Beam 2 (area B) on the valley floor, the rays will be more intense and so area A will be warmer than area B. As a result fields on the lower parts of south-facing slopes (e.g. area A) may be more suitable for growing crops than those on the valley floor since (i) they receive more direct sunlight and (ii) they are better drained and less subject to flooding. The fields on the valley bottom are therefore much more suitable for grassland e.g. for rearing cattle.
(d) In Scotland, the west coast has slightly higher winter temperatures than the east coast since the west is influenced more by warm south westerly winds which have been heated by the **North Atlantic Drift** — a current of warm water flowing from the Caribbean Sea north-eastwards to the shores of Western Europe. As a result there is less frost in the west and the growing season is longer (see Fig. 21).

3. Slope (gradient)

In many parts of Scotland (particularly in the Highlands and Southern Uplands), slopes are very steep. As a result the soil tends to be very thin since it is easily removed by wind and rainwater to the low-lying areas, which as a result have much thicker soils. It is also very difficult for machinery to be used on these steep slopes and so much of this land is used for the **rough grazing** of **hill sheep**. (See Fig. 28). There is however an increasing tendency to plant **forests** on such slopes since the trees (in addition to supplying wood) help to bind the soil particles together, protect it from the weather, and keep the soil relatively deep.

On less steep slopes farmers practise **contour ploughing** i.e. they plough along the contours rather than up and down the hillsides. This slows the flow of water down the hillside and reduces soil erosion. In more low-lying areas a gentle slope may be of benefit since the rainwater can run off it

Fig. 28   Rough grazing of hill sheep

easily while completely flat areas may have to be drained.

4. Soil type

Soil is a mixture of broken-down rock particles, living and dead organisms, air and water. It has **four** main characteristics of importance to the farmer (a) the amount of **nutrients** it holds, (b) its PH (whether it is acidic, alkaline or neutral), (c) its depth, and (d) the amount of water it holds. The best soils are deep, rich in nutrients, neutral or slightly alkaline and hold some but not too much water. These features are all greatly affected by climate, slope, underlying rocktype, the work of glaciers and rivers and the ways in which people have used the soil in the past. In general soils can be classified into three main types (see Fig. 29).

Fig. 29 shows that soils can be improved to some extent e.g. if it is dry water can be added to (irrigate) it, if it is too damp it can be drained. In addition **lime** can be added if it is too acidic and fertilizer if it lacks nutrients. Such measures are however expensive and so the changes the farmer can make are limited.

	Structure	Advantages	Disadvantages	Use by farmers
SANDY SOIL	Large particles and spaces	Retains little water so light and easy to plough– heats up quickly	Very dry. Water passes out easily taking nutrients with it	Arable farming if fertilised and watered (irrigated)
CLAY SOIL	Small particles and spaces	Retains water and nutrients	Retains water and so it is very heavy and difficult to plough and slow to heat up	Where adequate rainfall permanent grass for dairying. High crop yields if drained in areas of lower rainfall
LOAM SOIL	Mixture of particle sizes and space	Holds some but not too much water and holds nutrients	Few	Best soils— offer wide choice of uses

Fig. 29   Main soil types

Exercise

1 Give the meaning of the following terms in your own words:
arable farming   gradient   aspect   dairy cattle
permanent grassland

2 Explain the following statements in your own words:
(a) Scotland has a 'wetter west and a drier east',
(b) Altitude has a much greater effect on the growing season in Scotland than latitude,
(c) The growing season tends to be longer in western than in eastern Scotland.

3 Examine the sketch of a Highland valley (Fig. 30) and answer the following questions:
(a) Explain why most of the farms in this valley are likely to be on the **south-facing** slope,
(b) Give three reasons why area A may be more suited to the growing of cereals than area B,
(c) Suggest how the fields in area B may be better used,
(d) Suggest how the land on the **north-facing** slope may be used.

4 (a) Explain why soils on steep slopes tend to be very thin.
(b) Write down two ways in which the soil on such slopes can be deepened.

5 List the four characteristics of soil most important to farmers.

6 Describe and explain the advantages and disadvantages of having a field with **sandy** soil on a farm.

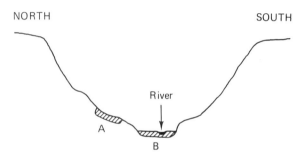

Fig. 30

B. Economic factors

Although the physical landscape sets limits to what is grown, the farmer's choice may further depend on three human (economic) factors, i.e. the government, the market and the farmer's assets.

1. The government

The government has a great influence on farmers in Scotland, since it may provide grants and tax relief to help pay for farm improvements like machinery, new storage facilities etc. It may also affect what is grown on the farm, by providing incentives to encourage the farmer to grow certain crops or rear certain animals which are needed by the country at any particular time. The government tries to encourage the production of as many types of crops and animals as

23

possible so that the country is not severely affected if imports from other countries are cut off for some reason.

2. The market

(Remember this does *not* simply mean a small livestock market held in a town square. The farm's market consists of anyone who will buy the produce of the farm.) Since most farmers are producing goods to sell they are affected by market demand, market price and the distance of their farms from the market.

(a) Market demand — the farmer must find someone willing to buy his products, e.g. a nearby brewery may provide a market for barley or a crisp manufacturer may want to buy potatoes. Market demand is largely affected by tastes i.e. what people like to eat and drink. In this country for instance there is a greater demand for cow's milk than goat's milk.

(b) Market price — the farmer will only grow crops or rear animals if he can get a good price for them. This is now greatly influenced by the E.E.C. (Common Market). Every year all the E.E.C. countries decide on a suitable price for each farm product so that farmers make a reasonable profit and trade between member countries is encouraged. Food imported from non-member countries is taxed, making it more expensive, so that farmers in the E.E.C. have an added advantage. If prices fall, due to a surplus of a product, the E.E.C. will buy the surplus and store it as far as possible until it is needed later — the surplus food is referred to as 'a mountain' e.g. there has already been a 'butter mountain'.

(c) Distance from the market — some crops e.g. fruit, vegetables and flowers, do not last very long once they are removed from the ground i.e. they are **perishable**. These crops must therefore be grown fairly near to their market so that they can be sold in fresh condition. Other crops which are less perishable and which are cheaper to transport e.g. cereals, can be grown much further from their market.

3. The farmer's assets

These are the money, machinery, workers, etc., he already has or could borrow. Some farm products are more expensive to produce than others. This may be due to the differing costs of seeds, the number of workers and machines needed and the amount of fertilizer required. Whether a farmer can afford these 'inputs' depends greatly on the **assets** he already has or could borrow. For example if a farmer cannot afford to buy the machinery or fertilizer necessary for growing wheat, he must borrow them, obtain a loan to buy them or carry out another type of farming which he can afford.

Exercise

1 Describe two ways in which the government can influence the products grown on a farm.
2 (a) Explain what is meant by a **market** for a farm's products.
   (b) Suggest three possible **markets** for a farmer rearing hill sheep.
   (c) Explain what was meant by the **butter mountain**, using the following words: E.E.C., surplus, store demand.

3 Explain what is meant by a farmer's **assets**.

Farming types

Farmers have to decide what crops to grow or animals to rear and, in order to make this decision, they must consider physical and human factors. This section deals with the effect these factors have on Scottish farmers in different parts of the country.

Look at Fig. 31. This is a general map showing the main types of farming in different parts of Scotland. It shows that farmers often make similar decisions in similar circumstances, e.g. many lowland farmers in East/Central Scotland concentrate on arable farming, while those in the west concentrate on dairy farming.

This does **not** mean however that the farms in each area produce **one product**. Very few

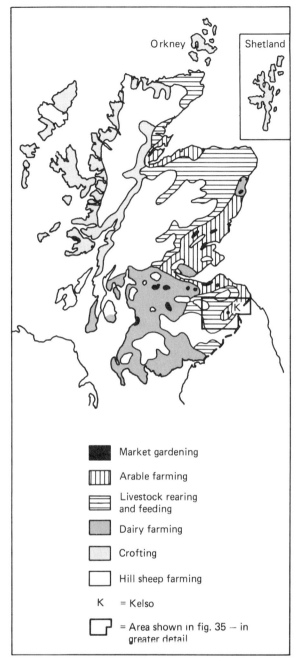

Market gardening

Arable farming

Livestock rearing and feeding

Dairy farming

Crofting

Hill sheep farming

K = Kelso

= Area shown in fig. 35 — in greater detail

Fig. 31   Farming types

farms have equal conditions of soil, slope, aspect, etc. in every field, and so the farmer will use different fields for different purposes in order to get the maximum benefit from the land. Furthermore, it would be an unwise

farmer who decided to put 'all his eggs in one basket' i.e. grow the same crop in each field, especially in a country where the weather is so unreliable. If the weather over the year did not suit the one crop grown the farmer could be ruined. As a result most Scottish farms tend to be **mixed farms** where the farmer relies on a variety of products. Fig. 31 then shows the **main** types of farming in each area, **not the only type.** Fig. 32 lists the six main types of farming activity in Scotland and their characteristics. The table also shows that farmers' decisions are greatly affected by the location of their farms. The most important influencing factors are listed in column D.

Exercise

1 Fig. 32 lists the main types of farming activity in Scotland, their characteristics and some of the main factors affecting their location. Copy the table then complete it by choosing the correct location for each type. Choose your answers from the following list:
    On slopes over 200 metres above sea level
    Coastal areas of the North West Highlands and Islands
    South West Scotland and areas surrounding large cities like Aberdeen
    Lower slopes of hillsides in Eastern Scotland
    East coast lowlands around Tweed Valley and Firths of Tay, Forth and Moray
    Scattered throughout Central Scotland, covering small areas only

2 List some of the reasons why:
    (a) Crofters cannot make a reasonable living from farming only and must take part-time jobs;
    (b) The main type of farming in West Central Scotland is dairy farming, while the main type in East Central Scotland is arable farming:
    (c) Large areas of the Highlands and Southern Uplands are used for sheep farming;
    (d) Livestock rearing farms are usually found higher up than arable farms.

3 What is meant by **crop rotation?** Find out as much about it as you can and explain why it is important to the farmer.

4 Many physical and economic factors are completely out of a farmer's control. Others however can be

25

A. Type of farming	B. Characteristics	C. Location	D. Some of the main factors influencing this location
1. Crofting	Part-time rearing of lambs and calves for sale to lowland farms		Found in isolated areas which are far from the main markets and have problems of heavy rainfall, steep slopes and thin acidic soils — these problems are so severe that another occupation is necessary
2. Hill sheep rearing	Sheep reared on hillside then sold to lowland farms for fattening		Another way of making money in areas with heavy rainfall, low temperatures, steep slopes and thin soils i.e. areas which are useless for other more profitable types of farming
3. Livestock rearing and feeding	Sheep and cattle (especially beef cattle) reared and fed on grass and cereals		Found in areas with lower rainfall and more sunshine i.e. areas where fodder crops like oats and barley grow well. Often 'pushed' on to higher land by more profitable arable farming
4. Dairy farming	Main activity is feeding cows on grass for the production of milk to supply dairies		Found in wetter lowlying areas (especially where there are clay soils) where rich grass can grow to feed dairy cattle. Usually found near to large towns and cities where fresh milk can be sold
5. Arable farming	Land ploughed for growing of crops like barley, wheat, potatoes, oats, sugarbeet for sale or for fattening livestock from uplands		Found in areas with lower rainfall and more sunshine — especially on lower flatter areas with deep, fertile soil
6. Market gardening (specialist farming)	Growing of 'perishable' produce (products which don't last long) e.g. fruit, flowers and vegetables in a small space often under glass		Found in areas near to large towns or cities where products can be sold or in areas which have a particularly favourable climate and soil type

Fig. 32

influenced to some extent. Consider the following three situations, each of which a farmer may face:

(i) Several low-lying fields contain excess clay and are frequently waterlogged,

(ii) The soil in one field is very acidic,

(iii) Some fields are exposed to strong winds from the south-west.

(a) Explain why each of these situations could cause problems.

(b) Suggest how these problems could be reduced or solved.

Fig. 33 illustrates a type of farming where the farmer influences his environment to a very great extent i.e. **specialised farming** or **market gardening**. Large market gardens are found near centres of high populations (see Fig. 31) and each may specialise in a particular fruit or vegetable e.g. those around Edinburgh specialise in vegetables and those around the Carse of Gowrie specialise in raspberries. Although this type of farming only requires a small area of land e.g. gardens, orchards or greenhouses, a great amount of care, work and money must be added and as a result high value products are yielded (see Fig. 34). This type of farming is described as **intensive**. Other types of farming which cover larger areas of land and which require less attention from the farmer are described as **extensive** e.g. hill sheep farming.

5 (a) Look at Fig. 33 and give three reasons why this is a good location for a **market garden**.

(b) Write an account, in about 150 words, describing and explaining ways in which the farmer has influenced the conditions in which crops are grown.

(c) Which of the six types of Scottish farming discussed best fits the term **extensive**? Explain your answer.

(d) Large market gardens such as those described above often encourage the growth of certain **industries** in the surrounding area. Suggest what two of these industries might be.

26

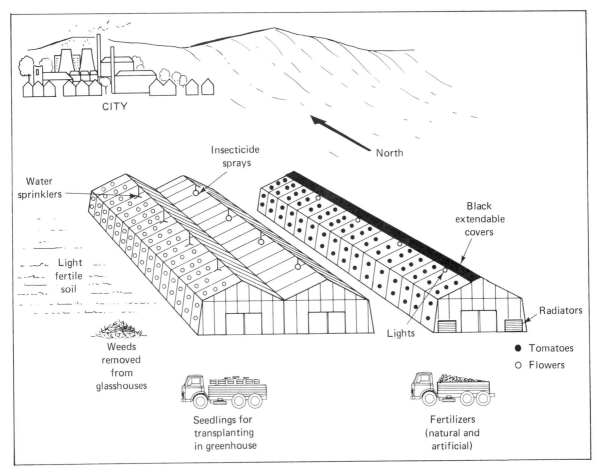

Fig. 33 Model of a market garden

Fig. 34 Tomatoes growing under glass

Upland and lowland farms in Scotland

As physical factors like rainfall, temperatures, soil and slope greatly influence land use and as these factors vary greatly between upland and lowland areas in Scotland it is not surprising that farm types differ also. A study of an upland farm and a lowland farm reveal some of these differences. Fig. 35 shows the position of two such farms in the Borders region of Scotland.

Rawburn — an upland farm

Rawburn Farm lies in the Lammermuir Hills 12 km north-west of Duns. As Fig. 36 shows, the land slopes steeply from the summit of Twin Law (447 m) to the valley of the Dye Water (at 220 m). The land available for farming on these slopes was reduced in 1954 when the Watch Water was dammed to produce the Watch Reservoir, so that some of the 730 mm of rain falling annually on these

27

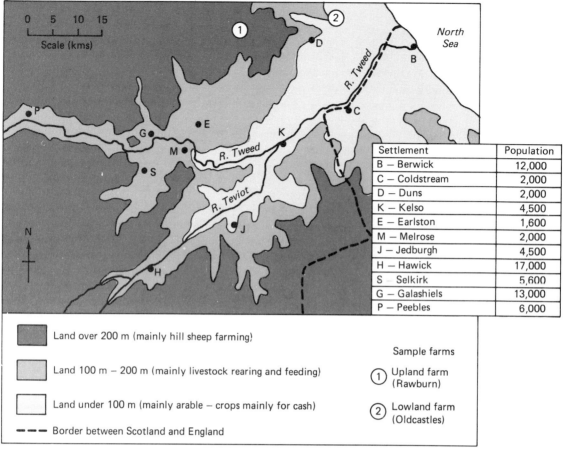

Fig. 35   Farming and settlement in the Tweed Basin

Settlement	Population
B — Berwick	12,000
C — Coldstream	2,000
D — Duns	2,000
K — Kelso	4,500
E — Earlston	1,600
M — Melrose	2,000
J — Jedburgh	4,500
H — Hawick	17,000
S — Selkirk	5,600
G — Galashiels	13,000
P — Peebles	6,000

hills could be stored and used to supply the towns of the Northern Tweed Basin with water.

Soils and land use

Of the 1904 hectares owned by the farmer today, 1524 hectares consist of exposed, unimproved steep hillside covered in acidic soil and heather moor (see Fig. 37). Such conditions are useless for cattle or arable farming and so the land is used for the rough grazing of 2800 Blackface and Cheviot sheep. In winter, conditions may be extremely harsh and sheep may be lost in snowdrifts on the hillside, so to prevent this happening they are usually brought down to ventilated buildings nearer the farm for shelter and feeding (see Fig. 38).

On the more sheltered, loam-covered slopes near the farmhouse is a smaller area of land which has been improved by the farmer.

Two-thirds of this is long term grassland where 100 home-bred (or home-reared) beef calves are grazed in the summer, (see Fig. 39) and the other one-third is **arable** land where barley, turnips, rape and hay (cut and dried grass) are rotated. These crops provide just enough food to feed the livestock in winter, although in extremely bad years, hay must be brought in from other farms. These harsh conditions do not allow large numbers of livestock to be fattened profitably on this farm, and so many of the calves and lambs are sold each year to lowland farmers for breeding or for fattening, before being slaughtered for beef and mutton. The high quality wool sheared from the Cheviot sheep is sold to local mills where it is woven into cloth while the poorer quality Blackface wool is used to stuff mattresses and to make carpets.

28

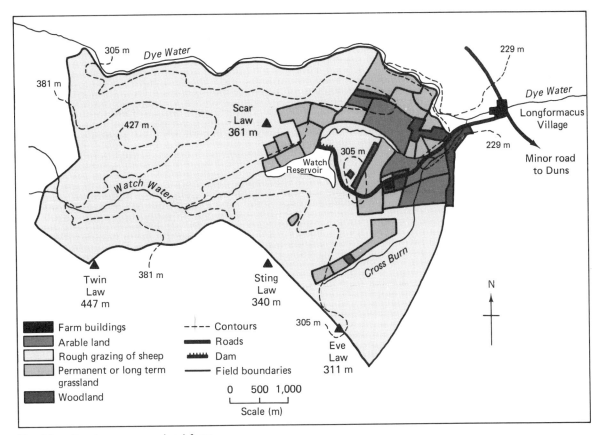

Fig. 36   Rawburn — an upland farm

Fig. 37

Labour
Seven people work all year round on the farm
— four of them as shepherds.

Machinery
In general the machines are fairly small, many
being quite old. The famer has 3 tractors,
1 JCB digger, 2 ploughs, 1 mower, 1 hay

Fig. 38

turner, 1 turnip harvester, 1 small baler and
1 bale transporter. There is no need for more
machinery on a livestock rearing farm such as
this.

Fig. 39

Oldcastles — a lowland farm

Oldcastles Farm (Fig. 40) lies in the Northern Tweed basin 9 km north-east of Duns. The land slopes gently from 125 m behind the farmhouse (see Fig. 41) to 74 m on the north and western boundaries of the farm.

Soils and land use

These gentle slopes allow the 630 mm of rain falling annually to drain away freely, but restrict the use of machinery very little and have allowed a deep loam soil to build up on

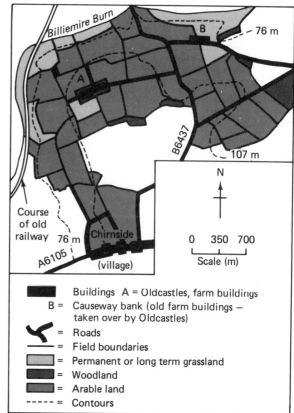

▇	Buildings A = Oldcastles, farm buildings
B =	Causeway bank (old farm buildings — taken over by Oldcastles)
⌐	= Roads
——	= Field boundaries
▨	= Permanent or long term grassland
▓	= Woodland
▒	= Arable land
- - - - -	= Contours

Fig. 40 Oldcastles — a lowland farm

Fig. 41

30

top of the sandstone beneath. Such conditions restrict farming to a much smaller degree than those on Rawburn and all of the 444 hectares have been improved by the farmer at some time. 387 hectares are **arable**, with barley and wheat being the main crops. Potatoes, peas, Brussels sprouts and grass are also grown in rotation (see Fig. 42).

All except the grass are **cash crops** i.e. they are grown for sale. The barley is sold to a distillery at Berwick, the wheat to an Edinburgh biscuit factory, the potatoes to a crisp manufacturer in Glasgow and the peas and sprouts to a processing and packaging company in Eyemouth.

Fig. 42

Most of the remaining 57 hectares consist of slightly steeper fields where 240 beef cattle (home-bred or bought from other farms) are grazed on permanent grass. During the winter these cattle are also fed indoors on silage

(preserved grass) and left-overs from the crops sold for cash, in order to fatten them for sale to slaughterhouses.

Labour
There are five permanent staff plus around 30 part-time labourers (brought in when extra workers are needed e.g. for harvesting potatoes and sprouts).

Machinery
In general the machines are much newer and much larger than those on Rawburn. The farmer has 8 tractors, 2 combine harvesters, 3 ploughs, 1 potato harvester, 1 stone separator, 1 forage harvester, 2 feeding trailers cultivating, sowing, spreading and spraying implements.

Exercise

1 Describe the role of crops on each of the two farms i.e. describe how each farmer uses his crops.

2 Examine the maps of Rawburn and Oldcastles Farms carefully and describe and explain the difference in the proportion of each farm used for **arable** farming.

3 Describe and explain the difference in size between the two farms.

4 'In general, upland farms in Eastern Scotland tend to rear livestock while lowland farms tend to prepare them for market'.
   (a) Explain the difference between 'rearing livestock' and 'preparing them for market'.
   (b) With references to Rawburn and Oldcastles explain the sentence above.

5 Look at Fig. 41. Why do you think the farmhouse is surrounded by trees?

6 Oldcastles has fewer full-time staff but in summer and autumn there are far more people working there than on Rawburn. Explain why.

Upland and lowland farms — a comparison

Although these two farms have features unique to themselves, they have many characteristics which are typical of other upland and lowland farms, particularly those in Eastern Scotland. We can therefore use them to compare upland and lowland farms in general.

Upland farms	Lowland farms

Fig. 43

Exercise

Choose which of the alternative statements below belong in each column of the table (Fig. 43), and copy the completed table into your jotter.
1 Found mainly in Central Scotland or coastal plains and river valleys elsewhere / Found in Highlands, Southern Uplands and low hills of Central Scotland

2 Usually very large / Usually smaller

3 Range in altitude usually less than 100 m / Range in altitude as much as 700 m

4 High percentage of land covered in bare rock or thin acid soil / High percentage of land covered in deep fertile soil

5 Growing season often less than 31 weeks due to low temperature / Growing season usually over 31 weeks due to higher temperatures

6 Mean annual rainfall can be under 700 mm / Mean annual rainfall usually above 700 mm

7 Good choice of land-use available / Poor choice of land-use available

8 Dominant land-use is rough grazing / Dominant land-use is permanent grassland (in west) arable (in east)

9 Most of farmland improved by farmer / Mostly unimproved

10 Livestock mainly for rearing / Livestock for fattening (in east) or milk production (in west)

11 Large number of workers (mainly seasonal) required / Few workers required

12 Large number of machines needed / Few machines needed

13 Boundaries made of local stone / Boundaries of hedges and fences

14 Crops usually all for fodder / Crops often for sale

3
The growth of towns (i)

Exercise

1 Examine Fig. 44 on p. 34. Then, using your atlas, copy and complete Keys 1, 2 and 3.

2 What do you notice about the location of the main settlements?

Nine hundred years ago there were no large towns in Scotland and most people lived in small farming villages. Today however most people live in the large towns or cities shown on Figs. 44 and 180 (p. 129). What are the reasons for this change?

The growth of market towns

One reason was that some villages became **market towns**. By the 18th century farming was becoming more and more efficient. Many new farming methods were introduced, machines were invented, new crops and animals were developed and many marshy areas were drained. As a result many villages began to produce more goods than they needed themselves and began to trade (or exchange) goods with another. Since this meant either having to walk or travel by horse and cart to another village the people usually decided to hold a market in the village which was most **accessible** i.e. easiest to get to.

In areas of flat fertile lowland villages were often evenly spaced as shown in Fig. 45. In such areas the most accessible village was the one nearest the centre (village 7). In Scotland however few areas are perfectly flat with no surface barriers, so the most accessible village often lay away from the centre, perhaps in a gap between hills or at a bridging point of a river. Around the square where the **market**

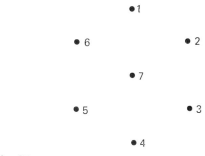

Fig. 45

was held, inns developed to provide food and shelter for the people coming in to trade. The goods brought into the market encouraged small scale **industries** to develop e.g. grain was ground to make flour and wool woven to make cloth. With the increase in farm machinery fewer people were needed to work on these farms and so many left the small villages to live in the market town and work as millers, bakers, brewers, weavers, blacksmiths, carpenters and cobblers i.e. all jobs essential to the growth of a town. All these incomers needed houses and market villages quickly grew into **market towns.**

Modern market towns

Today most people do not come to market towns to buy or sell livestock or grain, but to make use of the **services** which an accessible town usually provides for the people in the surrounding area. Such services include schools, shops, banks, cinemas, hospitals, lawyers, dentists and doctors. Small villages in the surrounding area are likely to have very few (if any) of these services and so people are drawn to the towns for them. As a result

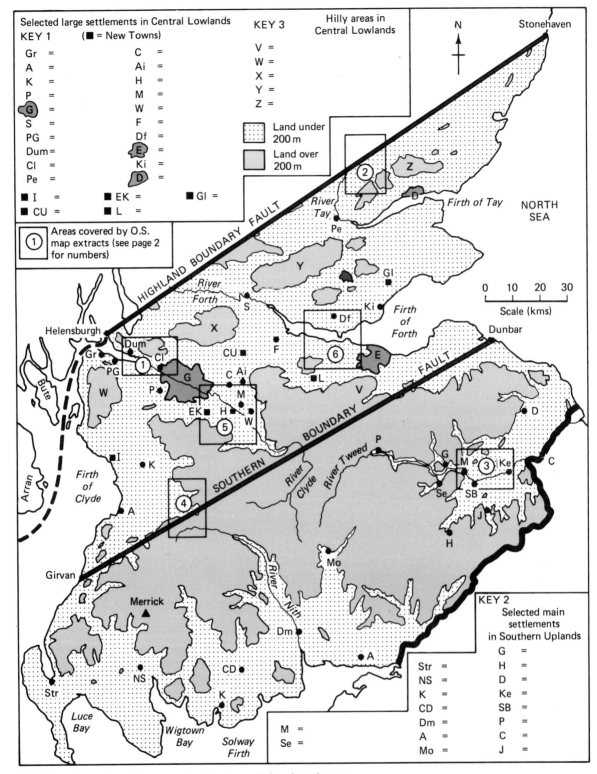

Fig. 44 Central and Southern Scotland — relief and settlement

The map contains the following keys and labels:

KEY 1 — Selected large settlements in Central Lowlands (■ = New Towns)

Gr = C =
A = Ai =
K = H =
P = M =
G = W =
S = F =
PG = Df =
Dum = E =
Cl = Ki =
Pe = D =

■ I = ■ EK = ■ Gl =
■ CU = ■ L =

① Areas covered by O.S. map extracts (see page 2 for numbers)

KEY 3 — Hilly areas in Central Lowlands

V =
W =
X =
Y =
Z =

Land under 200 m
Land over 200 m

KEY 2 — Selected main settlements in Southern Uplands

G = Str =
H = NS =
D = K =
Ke = CD =
SB = Dm =
P = A =
C = Mo =
J = M =
 Se =

Map labels: Stonehaven, N, NORTH SEA, Firth of Tay, River Tay, Pe, Z, D, Gl, River Forth, S, Ki, Firth of Forth, Dunbar, Helensburgh, Dum, Gr, Cl, PG, X, CU, F, Df, E, L, V, P, G, C, Ai, M, W, EK, H, D, Bute, W, I, K, G, Ke, C, Arran, Firth of Clyde, A, M, Se, SB, J, River Clyde, River Tweed, P, H, Girvan, Mo, Merrick, River Nith, A, Dm, CD, NS, K, Str, Luce Bay, Wigtown Bay, Solway Firth

HIGHLAND BOUNDARY FAULT, SOUTHERN BOUNDARY FAULT

Scale (kms): 0 10 20 30

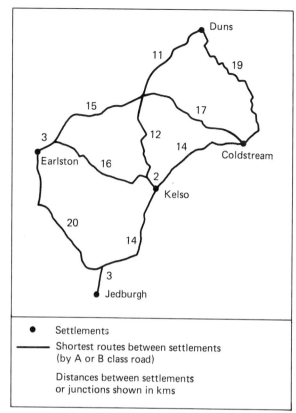

Fig. 46   Accessibility of settlements in middle Tweed Basin

Legend:

● Settlements

— Shortest routes between settlements (by A or B class road)

Distances between settlements or junctions shown in kms

settlements in that area. **A matrix** is a table for storing information in an orderly way e.g., in Fig. 48(a) A, B, C and D represent 4 villages connected only by 3 roads whose lengths are marked in kilometres. This information can be stored in the **accessibility matrix** Fig. 48(b) by carrying out the three steps indicated on the diagram.

Exercise

1 Use an **accessibility matrix** to find out which of the settlements on Fig. 47 is:
 (a) the **most accessible,**
 (b) the **least accessible.**

2 (a) Examine Fig. 46 showing selected settlements in the **Middle Tweed Basin** – distances shown are the shortest routes by A and B class roads. Use an accessibility matrix to work out which settlement is the most accessible.
 (b) Explain why this settlement developed into a **market town.**

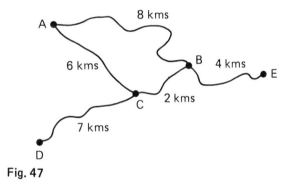

Fig. 47

many **market** towns have grown and developed as **service centres** with shops open six days a week replacing the old market held once a week. Some towns continue to hold regular markets but unless they also develop as a service centre or have other reasons for growth they remain fairly small.

Accessibility of settlements

Most **market towns or service centres** owe their continued growth to the fact that they are the most **accessible** town in the area. This does not always mean that they lie in the **middle** of that area but that they are easier to get to (particularly by road) than any other settlement.

One way of finding out which is the most accessible settlement in an area is to draw a table called an **accessibility matrix** using the shortest road distances between all the

Nodality of settlements – O.S. Map 3

The last exercise indicated a link between communications and the size of settlements. This can be shown in another way using a measurement called a **nodality index**. A settlement's nodality is a measurement of how well it is served by communications i.e. the **higher** the **nodality index** the more important the settlement is as a **route centre**. To calculate the **nodality index** of Earlston (square 5738) carry out the following four steps:

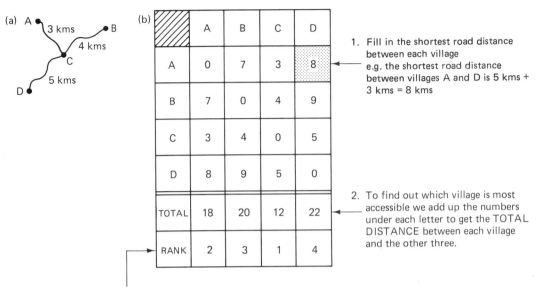

1. Fill in the shortest road distance between each village
e.g. the shortest road distance between villages A and D is 5 kms + 3 kms = 8 kms

2. To find out which village is most accessible we add up the numbers under each letter to get the TOTAL DISTANCE between each village and the other three.

3. Finally, we RANK the villages i.e. put them in order (1–4) with the village with the lowest total first. Since village C has the lowest total (12 kms) it is the MOST ACCESSIBLE

Fig. 48

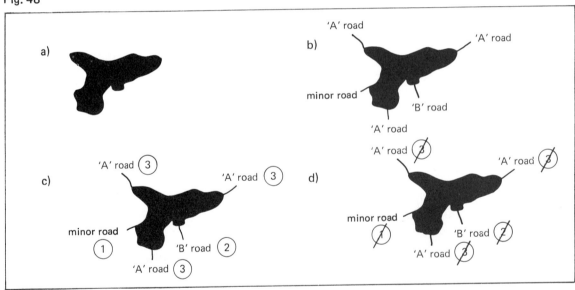

Fig. 49   Working out the nodality index

1. Place a piece of tracing paper over Earlston shade in the built-up area covered by the settlement (remember the built-up area is shown by grey buildings on older maps, pink on newer maps). (See Fig. 49(a).)

2. Trace on any transport route by which people may enter or leave the settlement. (See Fig. 49(b).)

3. Give each transport route a value i.e. a number of 'points' depending on how many people they bring in or out of the settlement in a given time. (See Fig. 49(c).)

A possible set of values is given below:

Motorway	4	Minor road	1
'A' class road	3	Car ferry	3
'B' class road	2	Passenger ferry	2

| Double track railway | 3 | Single track railway | 2 |

(Unless station is closed in the settlement.)
Note: It is important to make sensible sets of values e.g. motorways would always have more points than minor roads.

When comparing the nodality index of two settlements it is important to give routes the same value for each settlement.
4. Finally add up the total points – this will give you the **nodality index** for that settlement. (Tick or score out each number as you go round so that you do not miss any, see Fig. 49(d).)
∴ **Nodality index** of Earlston = 12

Exercise

O.S. Map 3
1 (a) Using this method calculate the **nodality index of Kelso** 7234 **Stichill** 7138 **Smailholm** 6436
(b) Which of the four settlements (including Earlston) has the highest nodality index?
(c) Referring to Fig. 35 and the O.S. map explain why this settlement has such a high nodality index compared with the other settlements.

2 (a) Copy and complete Fig. 50:
(b) Copy Fig. 51, of a simple **scatter graph** and plot these figures (Kelso has already been plotted for you). You should find that all the settlements lie within the dotted area on the scatter graph. This allows a **best fit line** to be marked, i.e. a line which indicates the **general relationship** between the **nodality** and **size** of a settlement.

3 Copy and complete the following sentence by choosing the correct word in capitals:
'In the case of the four settlements above the larger the settlement the GREATER / LESS the nodality index.'

A study of more settlements would reveal that this is a general rule but also that there are many exceptions to this rule e.g. some large settlements have a low nodality index (i.e. are not important as route centres) while other settlements are very small but have a high nodality index.

4 (a) Try to explain why larger settlements generally have a higher nodality index than smaller settlements.
(b) Using a selection of O.S. maps name some exceptions to this general rule and try to explain their unusual nodality.

Kelso — A market town and service centre in the Tweed Valley — O.S. Map 3

The Growth of Kelso

The location of a place can be described both in terms of its **site** and its **situation**. Its **site** is the actual piece of land it is built on while its **situation** is the wider area within which the site is found. Fig. 35 on p. 28 shows Kelso's **situation** while the O.S. map reveals more about Kelso's **site**. Fortunately Kelso had both an excellent **site** and **situation** for the development of an early market town.

Settlement	Size (km²)	Nodality index
Kelso		
Earlston		
Smailholm		
Stichill		

Fig. 50

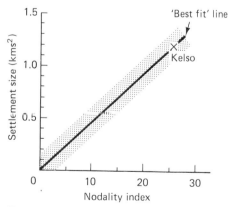

Fig. 51

Reasons for the growth of Kelso

Exercise

1 Using the following clues give seven reasons why a market town should develop at Kelso, i.e. three advantages of its **situation** and four advantages of its **site**.

Situation Clues

(a) The valleys of the River Tweed and Teviot on Fig. 35.

(b) Your answer to question 2a on p. 35.

(c) Its position in terms of the farming regions of the Tweed Basin (Fig. 35).

Site Clues (All on O.S. Map 3).

(a) The number of contour lines running through Kelso.

(b) Religious attraction at 730 337.

(c) River crossing at 727 336.

(d) Ancient defensive building at 711 347.

2 Can you suggest any more advantages of Kelso's site or situation which encouraged its growth?

3 By the 18th century a small market square had developed where local farmers sold their products.

(a) Give the six-figure grid reference of the most likely location for this square.

(b) Name one of the buildings bordering the square.

Fig. 52   Kelso grain mill

Fig. 53   Kelso market square today

38

Fig. 54 Aerial view of Kelso

4 (a) Eventually small agriculturally based industries developed in the town (see Fig. 52). What do you think an 'agriculturally based industry' is?
(b) Can you see any map evidence of such an industry in Kelso? (Give 6-figure reference.)
(c) Suggest a reason why this industry developed along the river.
(d) Name the feature on the river at reference 725 342.
(e) Can you suggest why it was built there?

5 'Few agricultural markets are held in old town squares today.' Examine Fig. 53 and describe how the old market square in Kelso is used now.

Modern Kelso

6 Examine the aerial photograph of Kelso (Fig. 54) and answer the following questions:
(a) In which direction was the camera pointing when the photograph was taken?
(b) Name rivers A and B.
(c) Name road C.
(d) What is building D?

(e) How might feature E have encouraged the growth of Kelso?

(f) Which of the two areas F and G is the older? Explain your answer.

7 (a) Copy the partially completed diagram below (Fig. 55) into your jotter (include title and key).

(b) Complete the 'Model of a market town' by arranging the features shown in the key in a sensible position.

(c) Explain the position you have chosen for the:
Market place;
New shopping area;
New Industrial Estate;
Routes taken by the roads and railway on your model.

(d) Try to explain the inclusion of a 'closed' railway station.

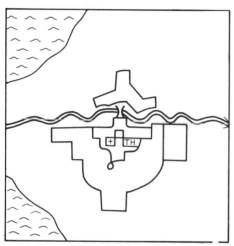

Key

■	= Market place (black)
⌒⌒	= Hills (grey)
▨	= New shopping area (orange)
TH	= Town Hall
▦	= Housing (yellow)
▤	= New industrial estate (purple)
⌇	= River (blue)
⊶O⊷	= Railway and station (closed)
⌇	= A class roads (red)
+	= Church
⠿	= Gently sloping farmland or other open space (green)

Fig. 55   Model of a market town

(a)

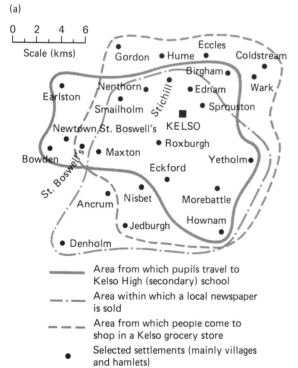

Scale (kms) 0 2 4 6

——— Area from which pupils travel to Kelso High (secondary) school

—·—·— Area within which a local newspaper is sold

— — — Area from which people come to shop in a Kelso grocery store

• Selected settlements (mainly villages and hamlets)

The sphere of influence of Kelso

The area which a settlement serves is called its **sphere of influence**. In order to measure the **sphere of influence** we choose some of the services it provides and find out the area each serves. For example, in Fig. 56(a), the area

(b)

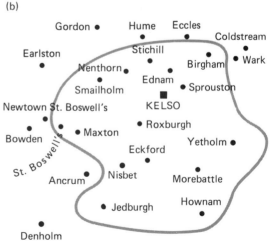

Fig. 56   General 'Sphere of Influence' of Kelso

served by the local newspaper, the secondary school and a large store in Kelso are shown separately. These can be used to make up a general map of Kelso's **sphere of influence**. Such a map is shown in Fig. 56(b).

Exercise

1 (a) What is meant by a town's sphere of influence?
(b) Suggest three other services which could be used to produce a map of the sphere of influence of any settlement.
(c) If you were asked to calculate the sphere of influence of your home town how would you go about this?

2 Kelso has more services than many other settlements of similar size in Scotland. Suggest a reason for this.

On p. 35 we discovered that Kelso was the most accessible town in the middle Tweed Basin by building up an **accessibility matrix**

using the shortest road distances. Distance however is not the only measure of accessibility. Another useful measure of the accessibility of a place is the time it takes to reach it. We can illustrate this by using an **isochrone** map such as the one in Fig. 57. **Isochrones** are lines joining points of equal time distance from a place. The map shows how accessible Kelso High School is to the pupils travelling there each day by school bus.

3 Examine Fig. 57 and answer the following questions:
(a) How long would it take pupils to reach school if they lived in St. Boswells?
(b) Using a ruler and the scale of the map calculate the distance from (i) Nenthorn and (ii) Birgham, to the school.
(c) Calculate the time of these two journeys.
(d) Using the map above explain your answer to c.
(e) Suggest why such a route is taken from Nenthorn when there is an A class road leading from there to Kelso.

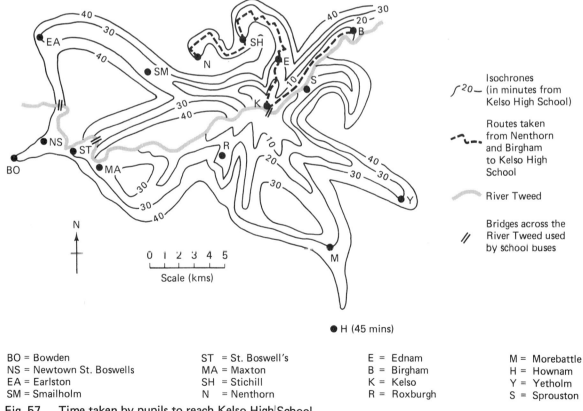

Isochrones
∫20— (in minutes from Kelso High School)

Routes taken from Nenthorn and Birgham to Kelso High School

River Tweed

Bridges across the River Tweed used by school buses

● H (45 mins)

BO = Bowden	ST = St. Boswell's	E = Ednam	M = Morebattle
NS = Newtown St. Boswells	MA = Maxton	B = Birgham	H = Hownam
EA = Earlston	SH = Stichill	K = Kelso	Y = Yetholm
SM = Smailholm	N = Nenthorn	R = Roxburgh	S = Sprouston

Fig. 57   Time taken by pupils to reach Kelso High School

(f) Calculate the average **speed** of the bus journey from Birgham to Kelso High School.

(g) Suggest why the isochrone lines stretch out 'arms' in various directions. (Refer to O.S. Map 3.)

The growth of industrial towns

The Woollen Industry in the Tweed Basin

An examination of Fig. 35 on p. 28 shows that Kelso is by no means the largest town in the Tweed Basin, e.g. Galashiels and Hawick have grown much larger. This is not because they are more important market towns, but because they became more important **manufacturing** towns where goods were made from local materials on a large scale. In the Tweed Valley this largely meant the production of woollen cloth using the abundance of wool from local sheep. At first most of the cloth was made by farming people in their spare time and in their own homes using hand-driven machines, i.e. the woollen industry at this time was merely a 'cottage industry'. Gradually, however, new, larger machines were invented which, when powered by **running water**, could do the work of several people in a much shorter time. As a result, many small factories (or mills) producing rough woollens developed along the River Tweed and its tributaries in the 18th and early 19th centuries. They used water for power and for washing and dyeing the wool.

The 19th century — Specialisation and growth

By the middle of the 19th century in Britain, **coal** was being burned to produce **steam** which could drive machinery more efficiently than running water could. Unfortunately there are no coalfields in the Tweed Basin and so the factories here could not produce cloth as cheaply as those which lay on or near coalfields (particularly those in Yorkshire) since the necessary coal had to be brought from elsewhere. In order to survive factories in the Tweed Basin had to **specialise** in (concentrate on) **high quality materials** for **export** to people who could afford to buy

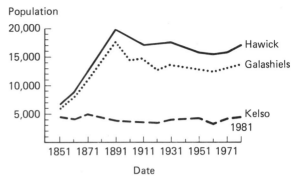

Fig. 58   Population change in selected Border settlements 1851–1981

them, e.g. in the U.S.A. and Central Europe. Many mills in **Galashiels** specialised in tweed — a high quality woven cloth, while those in **Hawick** specialised in high quality knitwear.

As a result these two towns grew rapidly in the 19th century as people who were no longer needed on the farms flocked in to look for work (see Fig. 58).

In order to make high quality goods the coarse wool from the Blackface sheep had to be replaced by finer wool from home-bred Cheviot sheep or wool imported from abroad. The building of a railway from Edinburgh to the south through the western Tweed Basin encouraged the growth of Hawick and Galashiels since coal and wool could be brought in and finished products sent out quickly by train.

The 20th century — New problems for the woollen industry

As Fig. 58 shows, the rapid growth in the population of Hawick and Galashiels came to a halt in the late 19th century and since then these towns have actually *lost* many people, (particularly the young). This change has resulted largely from changes in the woollen industry.

Although the development of electricity has brought cheaper power to the area, the industry has had to face many problems this century. There has been a fall in **market demand** for the area's products due to changes in fashion and increased competition, as other countries of the world are now producing

Fig. 59   Aerial view of Galashiels

high quality cloth and knitwear of their own
— often on newer more efficient machinery.

There has also been a **shortage** of **skilled labour.** Mechanisation has meant fewer jobs on farms and too few other industries have developed to provide work for local men so many have moved away with their wives (often skilled factory workers) and families to seek a job elsewhere. Many factories therefore had to close, leaving more people without jobs encouraging them to leave the area. This situation highlights the dangers of an area depending too much on one industry. When the industry faces problems the effects on the whole area can be devastating.

Possible answers?

The government and local authority realise that towns like Hawick and Galashiels have

Fig. 60   Inside a woollen mill

suffered from having 'too many eggs in one basket' and so have tried with the help of the Scottish Development Agency to remedy the situation.

One effort has been to attract **many different types** of new industry into the area by building new factories on new estates and offering loans or rent-free periods to industrialists willing to start up in the area.

Another scheme has involved the building of a completely new settlement called **Tweedbank** between Melrose and Galashiels. When complete it will have a similar structure to the 'New Towns' of Central Scotland but on a much smaller scale. (See Fig. 61.)

The housing estates will be separated from the industrial estate by 'green areas' of trees, shrubs and grassed open spaces. There will be a traffic-free central shopping area and adequate community facilities like schools, a health centre, youth clubs and playing fields will be provided. Hopefully, such a pleasant environment will attract young people into Tweedbank and so provide a labour force for industries attracted to the new industrial estate.

Although such measures are having some success and industries like electronics and surgical instruments and sports goods manufacturing have been attracted to the area (see Fig. 62), the population of the Upper Tweed Basin continues to decrease. It is clear that efforts to attract more people back into the area to live and work must continue.

Exercise

1 List as many reasons as you can why the **woollen industry** developed along the River Tweed and its tributaries.

Fig. 61   Tweedbank

Fig. 62   Manufacturing surgical instruments

2 (a) What is meant by 'specialisation' of an industry?
  (b) Explain why the woollen industry had to become much more specialised in the 19th century.

3 (a) Explain why large numbers of people have been leaving the Tweed Basin this century.
  (b) What measures have been taken to reverse this situation.

Although in the 19th century the industrial towns along the upper reaches of the River Tweed grew much larger than the market centres or agricultural settlements further down, they are still very small compared with the towns and cities of the Central Lowlands (see Fig. 6). We shall discover some reasons for this in Chapter 4.

4

The growth of towns (ii)

Today, Glasgow is Scotland's largest city, with a population of 747 000 inhabitants. This, however, has not always been the case.

Before 1300 — A market and religious centre

During the 5th century AD Glasgow was only one of the many small settlements along the **River Clyde** (see Fig. 63), but since then it has grown remarkably, outstripping every other

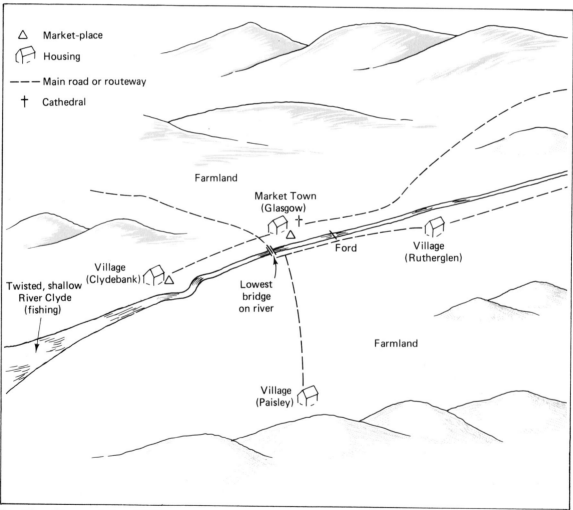

Key:

△ Market-place

⌂ Housing

- - - Main road or routeway

† Cathedral

Farmland

Market Town
(Glasgow)

Ford

Village
(Rutherglen)

Village
(Clydebank)

Twisted, shallow
River Clyde
(fishing)

Lowest
bridge
on river

Farmland

Village
(Paisley)

Fig. 63   Glasgow before 1300

settlement in Scotland. The Clyde was shallow enough at Glasgow to be forded (crossed) by people travelling north or south across Scotland, so a main north-south routeway developed, passing through the settlement. When a **bridge** across the river was built this routeway became even more important.

To the north of the river there is a **high ridge** which provided a good site for a **fort**, as well as a small settlement (under the fort's protection) away from the floodwaters of the river. It was inhabited by fishermen, farmers and a few craftspeople. In the 6th century the settlement became known as a holy place, since it was said to be the chosen home of St. Mungo. As a result a church (which later became a cathedral) and a university were built.

In the 12th century Glasgow, unlike many surrounding settlements, obtained the right to hold a **market**. Since rules about buying and selling goods were very strict at the time, the people from surrounding areas had to come to Glasgow to trade bringing wealth and encouraging growth. Despite all these advantages the population was still under 2 000 by AD 1300.

1300—1800 A port and textile centre

Gradually Glasgow's merchants became more and more powerful as home and foreign trade increased until Glasgow became the richest

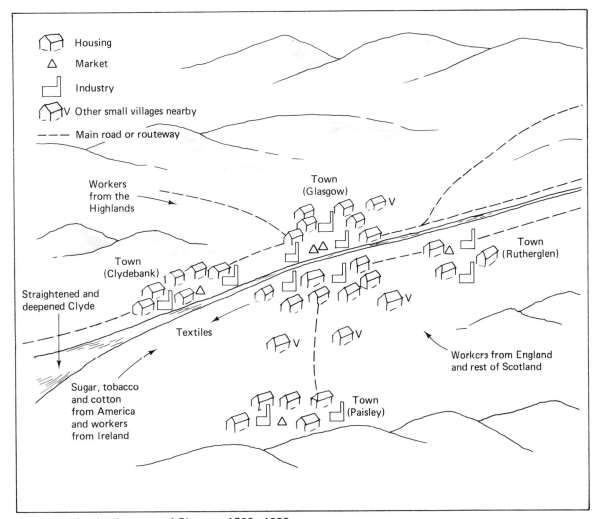

Fig. 64   The development of Glasgow, 1300—1800

burgh on the Clyde and a hive of 'cottage' industry (see Fig. 64). It would have developed even more quickly but for two problems:

1. The Clyde was too shallow for large boats and many small islands broke it up into several twisting channels, so cargo destined for abroad had to be carried overland to Irvine or, (later) by small boats, to a new harbour at Port Glasgow, then transferred to larger ships for export.

2. Being on the west coast, Glasgow faced away from the main trading ports of Europe. The first problem was reduced greatly however, in the late 1700s when great efforts were made to deepen and straighten the river allowing larger ships to reach Glasgow. Furthermore,

the west coast location became a great advantage when after 1707, Glasgow was allowed to trade with the American colonies. Sugar, cotton and (especially important) tobacco were imported and sold to Europe by Glasgow's merchants and products like textiles and leather goods were made in the town. Such activities brought great wealth to Glasgow.

In the late 18th century cotton replaced tobacco as the main import. Newly invented machines were used to manufacture textiles and water-powered factories were built to manufacture these goods on a large scale. Thousands of people, not only from around Glasgow but from the Highlands, Ireland and

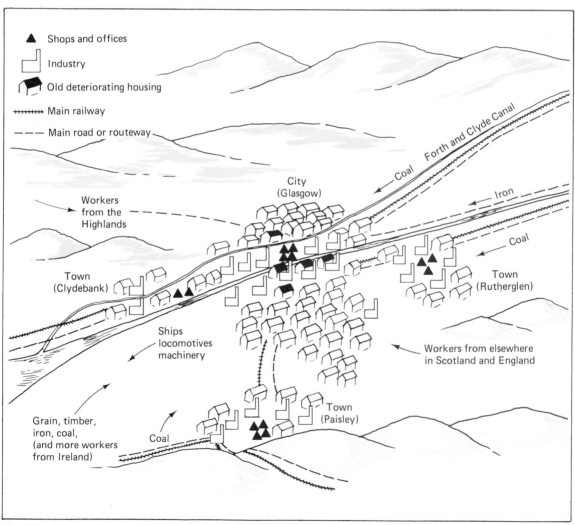

Fig. 65   The development of Glasgow, 1800–1945

48

England, came to live and work in the town and by 1800 the population was over 70 000.

1800–1945 A centre of 'heavy industry'

By the late 18th and early 19th centuries a period which became known as the **Industrial Revolution** had arrived. During this time industrial development in Scotland increased at a fantastic rate, due largely to two achievements:
1. The discovery and development of processes for producing **large amounts of iron** cheaply, using **coal** as a raw material.
2. The application of the much more efficient coal-burning **steam engine** to **machinery** and to **transport** by **rail** and **sea**. Once again Glasgow's location proved fortunate (unlike that of the towns of the Tweed Basin) since the city lay on a **coalfield** and near to iron ore deposits. The deepening of the River Clyde continued, then **canals** (like the **Forth** and **Clyde Canal** – 1790) and later **railways** were developed to transport these raw materials in and manufactured products out. As a result Glasgow rapidly became a centre of **'heavy' industries** like iron making, shipbuilding and engineering, producing **heavyweight products** for an ever-increasing world market (see Fig. 65). Hundreds of thousands of people flocked to Glasgow in search of work in these industries and the population grew at an incredible rate, until the peak around the middle of this century when well over one **million** people lived within the city boundaries.

The city also developed as an important service centre, but unlike Kelso which merely serves a small rural area, Glasgow's 'sphere of influence' stretches across most of Scotland. providing huge department stores, hospitals, universities, theatres and cinemas. Furthermore the headquarters of businesses like industrial firms, banks and lawyers all lie near the city centre.

Thousands upon thousands of new houses were built and Glasgow grew in all directions swamping surrounding villages, towns and farmland until it became the 'Second city of the British Empire'.

Exercise

1 Look at Fig. 66. All the features in column A have had a significant effect on Glasgow's growth. Column B explains why these features have had such an effect. The statements in column B are however in the wrong order. Write out twelve **proper sentences** beginning with the statements in column A and containing the statements in column B in the correct order e.g. The River Clyde provided fish and freshwater early on and later provided an important routeway for Glasgow's imports and exports.

Modern Glasgow – a changing city

Fig. 67 shows that Glasgow's population increased rapidly for well over 100 years reaching a peak around the middle of this century. This rapid increase left the city with many problems. These problems can be divided into three groups:
1. Housing
2. Transport
3. Unemployment

Glasgow's housing problem
Glasgow's population grew at a tremendous rate during the 19th and early 20th centuries as people came into the city looking for work in the growing **heavy** industries. At this time only the very rich had private transport and public transport was limited, so most people had to walk to work. As a result thousands of three or four storey houses called **tenements** were rapidly built in rectangular blocks close to the docks and factories near the city centre (see Fig. 68 and Fig. 77 on page 56). Since they had to be built so quickly and close together, many of these tenements were more like shelters than homes. Only very basic facilities were provided. In the worst areas a whole family could live in a single room, while a dozen or so families living in each 'close' (i.e. the homes with doors opening on to the shared staircase or 'landing'), shared a 'back court' which had one toilet, one washing house and a clothes-drying area and formed the only play area (other than the streets) for children. The rooms were usually dark, damp and airless and with the overcrowded insanitary

A	B
1. The River Clyde provided	A. provided armed protection against attack for the small growing settlement
2. The ford and bridge	B. allowed larger vessels to reach Glasgow
3. The high ridge	C. provided raw materials for the development of "heavy" industry
4. The fort	D. encouraged people from surrounding areas to come to Glasgow to trade or even live
5. The market	E. provided a lookout site away from floodwater
6. The west coast location	F. fish and freshwater early on and later provided an important routeway for Glasgow's imports and exports
7. The deepening of the Clyde	G. provided a place of employment for thousands of people entering the town
8. The importing of cotton	H. was an advantage Glasgow had over eastern ports when trade with America became important
9. Factories, dockyards and industrial works	I. encouraged the development of the textile industry and the growth of the port in the 18th C.
10. The coal and ironfields	J. encouraged a North to South routeway through Glasgow in early times
11. The Forth and Clyde canal	K. powered machinery, trains and ships and so greatly encouraged their development
12. The steam engine	L. provided an important routeway for the transport of raw materials and manufactured goods from east to west Scotland

Fig. 66   Factors encouraging the growth of Glasgow

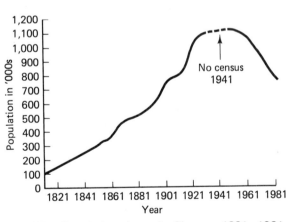

Fig. 67   Population change in Glasgow, 1821—1981

conditions, diseases like cholera and typhus spread rapidly. The unhealthy conditions were made worse by the smoke, dust and other chemical pollutants which were spilled into the air by the nearby factories. As time passed the houses grew older and older and living conditions deteriorated.

In an attempt to reduce this terrible problem, thousands of new houses (including new tenements) were built on the outskirts of the town as more efficient methods of transporting people developed i.e. the horse-bus, the tram and later the railway, allowing people to live further away from their work. Massive attempts were also made to improve the older houses in the centre by installing hot water, baths, larders, drying facilities, and ventilation among other amenities. Despite these tremendous efforts, however, **one seventh** of the population of Scotland was still squeezed into seven square kilometres (the centre of Glasgow) by the end of the Second World War.

Fig. 68   Inner city housing. Glasgow 1897

To make matters worse the four lowest bridges on the Clyde crossed the river near the city centre (see Fig. 70) and so the main road network brought thousands of vehicles into the city centre each day to use these bridges e.g., people travelling from Greenock to Helensburgh (on the opposite bank of the Clyde) had to make the huge detour through Glasgow. Of all the traffic entering the city centre only about one half wished to stop there — the rest merely needed a crossing point.

Such congestion lead to wasted time and fuel and to increased numbers of accidents, especially since many pedestrians crossed the busy roads all day long. This problem increased rapidly since more and more people were able to buy cars and industries came to depend more and more on **road** transport rather than on railways.

Unemployment
During its rapid growth Glasgow had depended

Fig. 69   Argyle Street, Glasgow 1930

Transport — congestion
Fig. 69 shows a street in the centre of Glasgow in 1930. The city centre had become increasingly overcrowded, not only by people but by transport vehicles like buses, trams and cars, as the city's population and importance as an industrial and service centre increased.

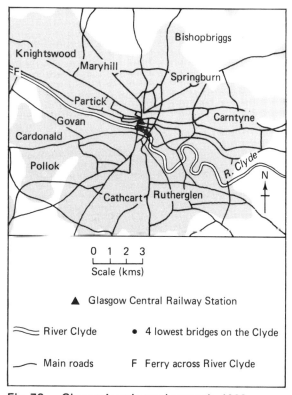

Fig. 70   Glasgow's main road network, 1960

too much on **heavy** industries like steelmaking, heavy engineering and shipbuilding. Unfortunately, most of these industries have declined leaving many people without a job.

Fig. 71

How have these problems been solved?

Four major solutions have been attempted:

1. The construction of large housing schemes and industrial estates on the outskirts
Firstly people had to be moved out of the city centre and provided with houses and jobs. In the 1950s huge housing schemes like Castlemilk, Easterhouse and Drumchapel were built on the outskirts of the city providing homes for 100 000 people, mainly in the

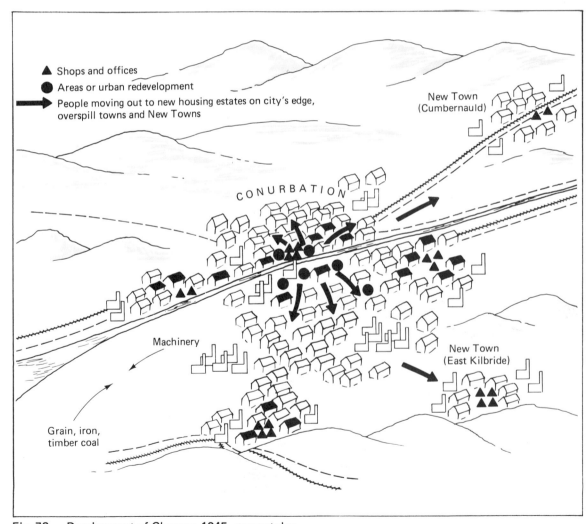

Fig. 72   Development of Glasgow, 1945–present day

Fig. 73

form of three or four storey flats (see Fig. 71 and Fig. 72).

New industrial estates like Hillington and Queenslie were also built on the outskirts (but separate from the housing), in an attempt to attract new industries and to provide jobs for the people of the city. The factories on these estates produce a large **variety** of **lightweight products** and use **electricity** as their power source, thereby polluting the atmosphere to a much smaller extent than older works.

2. Urban renewal (urban redevelopment) – the process of modernising an old area of a city.

In the 1950s planners identified the areas with the most severe housing problems and called them **Comprehensive Development Areas** or C.D.A.s e.g. the Hutchesontown/Gorbals C.D.A. on the south bank of the Clyde. The people living in these areas were moved out then bulldozers were sent in to demolish all the old buildings. Gradually the area was rebuilt with new houses, shops and schools laid out at lower densities i.e. with much more open space between them. Most industries were moved away from the houses often to estates on the outskirts of the city.

The new houses all had indoor toilets and modern household facilities. Many were in 2–5 storey blocks while others were in **multi-storey blocks** (Fig. 73). These multi-storeys were thought necessary since the demand for homes was enormous but the groundspace very limited. Urban renewal has also involved great changes to the city's transport network, i.e. its roads and railways. Two major plans have been developed for such renewal i.e. the **Glasgow Highway Plan** (Fig. 74) and the **Clyderail Plan.**
The Highway Plan
This has involved:
– the construction of **radial** (spoke like) **motorways** and **expressways** to allow quick travel in and out of the city centre. **Motorways** are wide roads with several

53

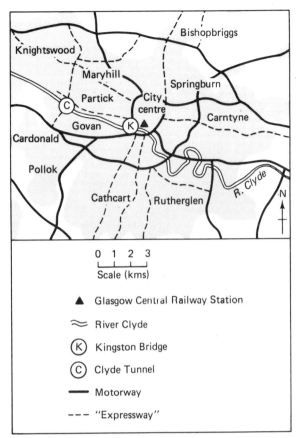

Fig. 74 Glasgow's Highway Plan

Scale (kms)

▲ Glasgow Central Railway Station

≈ River Clyde

Ⓚ Kingston Bridge

Ⓒ Clyde Tunnel

— Motorway

--- "Expressway"

Fig. 75 The Kingston Bridge

lanes and certain restrictions to allow rapid traffic movements e.g. no U-turns, no stopping and no bicycles, mopeds or pedestrians are allowed on them. Any road crossing their path does so at a different level using **flyovers** (see Fig. 75) and traffic must enter or leave the motorway via **slip lanes** on the left-hand side. **Expressways** are 'almost motorways' but they have fewer lanes and fewer restrictions;

— the construction of **inner** and **outer ring roads** to allow traffic to by-pass the city centre and so reduce congestion there;

— the use of **one-way streets** in the centre to allow more traffic through in one direction.

— the separation of traffic and pedestrians using **flyovers, under-passes** and **pedestrian precincts** i.e. streets where the only vehicles allowed are **emergency vehicles** like police cars, ambulances and fire engines or vans supplying shops and offices (see Fig. 76);

— the blocking of roads forming **cul-de-sacs** (particularly in redeveloped housing areas).

This cuts out through-traffic and makes these areas safer for pedestrians;

— an increase in car park space, often by the construction of **multi-storey car parks**.

The River Clyde has been a barrier to road transport so has contributed greatly to the congestion. This barrier has been overcome to a large extent by the construction of the **Clyde Tunnel** and **Kingston Bridge** (see Fig. 75), although the **Erskine Bridge** much further downstream has been of only limited help in solving the problem.

The Clyderail Plan

This has involved:

— the extension, electrification and modernisation of railway lines and stations in and around the city;

— the modernisation of the underground system;

— the **linking** or **integration** of the railways,

Fig. 76   Pedestrian precinct in Glasgow

underground, bus services and car parks, so
that people can move from one part of the
city to another in the quickest possible
time, perhaps leaving their car in a car park
on the outskirts and travelling in to the city
centre by rail, bus or underground.

3. Overspill Towns

The process of changing the face of the city
itself could not solve Glasgow's problems on
its own. People had to be encouraged to leave
the city altogether to make way for
redevelopment. One method of doing this
involved 'Glasgow overspill' agreements where
smaller settlements around Scotland were
given housing and industrial grants if they
were willing to provide homes and jobs for
the people moving into their towns from
Glasgow. Many people finding work in these
towns were then provided with a house, thus
relieving much of the population pressure on
the city.

4. New Towns

Another solution involved the construction of
completely 'New Towns' on sites throughout
Central Scotland. Five such New Towns have
been built and each has played an important
part in providing homes and jobs for people
willing to leave Glasgow.

Local Plans

Fig. 67 on p. 50 illustrates the success of the
measures taken to reduce the problems of
overcrowding in the city. Glasgow's population
has declined from well over **one million** in
1945 to under 750 000 today. This success
however has been at a cost. Where efforts in
the past were directed towards providing
decent houses for the city's people to live in,
either within redevelopment areas or on huge
council housing estates (like Castlemilk) on
the outskirts, the city authorities failed to
provide enough **variety** in housing types and
enough **amenities** like shops, health centres
and leisure facilities. Furthermore the people
being moved to new housing areas had little
say in how their new home area should look
and so took very little pride in it at all finding
that the 'community spirit' of the old
tenements was lacking.

Glasgow has been less successful than the
New Towns and other towns in Scotland in
attracting new industry so unemployment has
remained very high. As a result of these
problems **too many** people (many being
young skilled workers) are now leaving the
city and there is a real danger that whole
communities in Glasgow could die out leaving
households stranded among deserted housing
schemes. Since 1972 however, there have
been great efforts to change this situation.
The city has been divided up into several
Local Areas and future developments within
each area will be based on **local plans**. Great
efforts are now being made to involve local
people in shaping their future environment.

One area where the loss of population has
been particularly worrying is the East End of
the city and as a result a project called the
Glasgow Eastern Area Renewal Project (or

G.E.A.R.) has been set up. A variety of new houses, shopping centres, health centres and leisure facilities have all been built and the environment 'landscaped' with parklands, grassed play areas and tree-lined walk-ways in order to improve the quality of life in this part of the city. In an effort to create new jobs for the people, new factories and workshops have been built and loans, advice and rent-free periods offered to industrialists willing to start a business in this area. In addition, people are trained for work at new skill centres and training centres so that they have a better chance of a job when one becomes available. This type of **urban renewal**, unlike the renewal of the 1960s and early 70s, is designed to attract young people back into the city to live — without of course, ever allowing it to become **overpopulated** again.

Glasgow — land use zones

Glasgow, like the other cities in Scotland, has been involved in massive efforts to solve the many problems created by its rapid growth. The face of Glasgow has improved immensely since the Second World War and the standard of living has been raised greatly. Nevertheless differences in living standards and the quality of housing still exist and certain **urban zones** have developed, as shown in Fig. 77.

The city has developed around its **Central Business District** or CBD (the main area of shops and offices) on the north bank of the Clyde. Around this, extending along the river, and northward along the old Forth/Clyde and Monkland Canals is the zone of old, poorer quality houses (many being tenements) intertwined with old industrial works, docks and factories. Most of the areas undergoing **urban renewal** are found here since these are the areas in greatest need of change.

To the south and west of these zones much more time and effort was put into the building of higher quality houses extending out in wedges from the city centre. These locations ensured that the **southwesterly** prevailing winds would not blow industrial fumes over the houses. These houses, although fairly old now, are still of good quality and are owned by some of Glasgow's wealthier citizens.

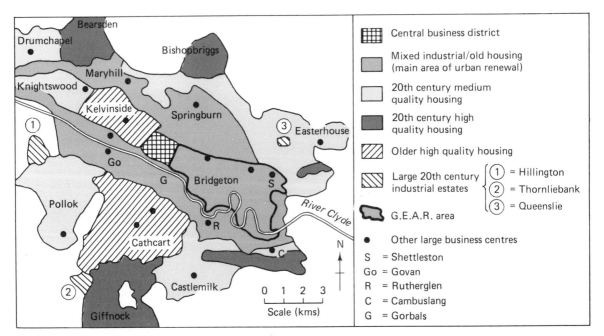

Fig. 77   Glasgow's urban zones

Fig. 78

Further out from the centre are the newer council housing estates, built to reduce the overcrowding in the Inner City earlier this century (see Fig. 71). On the outskirts of the city and on estates just outside its boundary are spacious modern private houses i.e. houses owned by people who can afford to buy them and to live far from the city centre (Fig. 78).

Also on the outskirts, but separate from the housing areas, are the newer industrial estates manufacturing many kinds of lightweight products and providing employment for many of the city's people. Throughout the city are smaller **Business Districts**, surrounded by smaller areas of older housing and industry. Many of these grew up as small villages or towns, which have since been 'swallowed up' by the city.

Exercise

1 Examine Fig. 68 on p. 51.
  (a) Name the type of building shown. *1 mark*
  (b) Explain why thousands of these buildings had to be built in a very short time during Glasgow's history. *2 marks*
  (c) Explain why such blocks of buildings became extremely unhealthy to live in the early years of this century. *3 marks*
  (d) Most of these buildings were built very near to docks, factories or industrial works. Explain why. *1 mark*

2 'Much of the **urban renewal** which has taken place in Glasgow has been in the area around the Central Business District and along the River Clyde'.

(a) What is meant by **urban renewal**? *1 mark*
(b) Explain the statement above in your own words. *2 marks*

3 Fig. 73 shows some of the houses which have replaced those in Fig. 68 in one of the redeveloped areas of Glasgow.
  (a) List as many features as you can which make this area much more pleasant to live in now. *3 marks*
  (b) Explain why the construction of multi-storey flats was thought to be necessary. *1 mark*
  (c) Suggest some of the advantages and disadvantages of living in such high buildings. *3 marks*

4 After the Second World War thousands of people from the inner city were encouraged to move to huge housing estates on the edge of the city in an attempt to reduce overcrowding.
  (a) Name two of these large housing estates in Glasgow. *2 marks*
  (b) Although these estates provided a much higher standard of living than the inner city areas, many people were at first unwilling to move out to live in them. Explain why. *2 marks*

5 There are of course many areas of beautiful housing in Glasgow as Fig. 78 shows.
  (a) Describe the houses shown on the photo. *1 mark*
  (b) What does this suggest about the income of the people living here. *1 mark*
  (c) Suggest where in Glasgow you might find such houses. *1 mark*

6 Examine the graph (Fig. 67) on page 50, then:
  (a) Describe the changes in Glasgow's population
    (i) between 1820 and 1951; *1 mark*
    (ii) between 1951 and 1981. *1 mark*
  (b) Explain your answer to part (ii) using the terms 'overcrowding', 'overspill towns' and 'New Towns'. *3 marks*

7 In an attempt to reduce Glasgow's unemployment problems, new industrial estates have been built, particularly near the outskirts of the city.
  (a) Name two of these estates. *2 marks*
  (b) An increasing number of Glaswegians are employed in **service** industries such as the one illustrated by Fig. 79.
    (i) Which industry is illustrated by this photograph? *1 mark*
    (ii) Where in Glasgow would you expect this photograph to have been taken? *1 mark*
    (iii) Explain your answer to (ii). *1 mark*

Fig. 79

8 (a) Explain what is meant by the 'Glasgow Highway Plan' (*1 mark*) then state how the development of such a plan has been of benefit to:

(i) People driving straight through Glasgow; *1 mark*

(ii) People driving into the city centre; *1 mark*

(iii) People shopping in the city centre; *1 mark*

(iv) People raising a family in houses near the city centre. *1 mark*

(b) Explain why the Kingston Bridge (Fig. 75) has played an important part in the development of this plan. *1 mark*

(c) Explain in your own words what is meant by the 'Clyderail' plan and describe the benefits it has brought to Glasgow. (See Fig. 80.) *3 marks*

9 (a) Explain what is meant by a **Local Plan**. *1 mark*

(b) Explain why such Local Plans are expected to give people more pride in their local area. *1 mark*

10 (a) Explain what is meant by the G.E.A.R. project. *1 mark*

(b) What effect is this project likely to have on the population of the East End of Glasgow. *1 mark*

(c) Explain how the planners hope to achieve this change. *3 marks*

Total 50 marks

Fig. 80

Models of city growth

Many people think of a city as a large 'tangled mass of buildings each with a different function,' and with no plan or logic behind its growth. A study of the structure of many cities, however, reveals that this is not the case. Most cities tend to develop several **functional zones** i.e. areas where buildings built for a similar purpose tend to group together in a particular part of the city, e.g. shops are usually found together, as are new houses and new factories – they are seldom mixed up nowadays, but arranged in functional zones within the city.

Geographers in the past have studied these zones in many cities and have found that the zones are arranged in a similar way in different cities. Some have produced models which they think best illustrate how these zones are arranged. The following are three such models.

Key (for 3 models)

■ Central business district

▨ Twilight zone

▦ Medium quality housing

▨ High quality housing

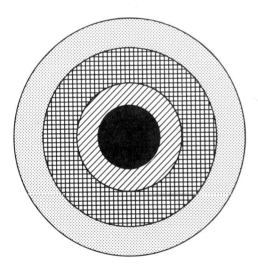

As the city grows the zones move outwards continually replacing the zone to their outside

Fig. 81   Concentric model

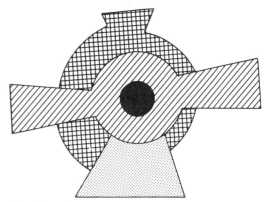

Fig. 82   Sector model

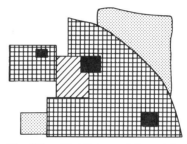

Fig. 83   Multiple nuclei model

1. Concentric model (Fig. 81)

This model is based on the idea that a city develops outwards from its centre to form a series of circular zones. At the centre is a **Central Business District** (CBD) of shops and offices. Around this a **twilight zone** or transitional zone develops containing older, poor quality housing mixed with industrial works and factories. Many of the houses may be in the process of conversion into shops or offices, while others would be deteriorating into slums. Around this would be a zone of newer **medium quality housing** followed by a zone of **high quality housing** on the outside.

2. Sector model (Fig. 82)

This model is based on the idea that different land uses arising near the centre of the city tend to grow outwards in wedges as the city gets larger e.g. if a zone of high class housing develops on one side of the CBD it will grow outwards wedged between other zones.

It also recognises that transport routes like roads, rivers, railways and physical features like steep hills have a great effect on land use,

59

e.g. the twilight zone may develop along the river.

3. Multiple nuclei model (Fig. 83)

This model is based on the idea that different land uses in the city tend to develop around certain growing points or **nuclei** e.g. small nuclei of shops may be dispersed throughout the city to serve surrounding housing areas with goods they need to buy every day e.g. small grocers or newsagents.

Note: None of the creators of these models expect their model to fit every city exactly — but they do feel that most cities show the characteristics illustrated by their model.

Exercise

1 (a) Compare Glasgow with each of these models by copying and completing the table below (Fig. 84).
   (b) Which model most closely resembles the city of Glasgow?
   (c) Describe and try to explain the location of:
   (i) old industrial areas (twilight zone);
   (ii) medium class housing;
   (iii) high-class housing estates;
   (iv) small shopping centres;
   (v) the C.B.D. — in the city of Glasgow.

Model	Similarities between model and Glasgow	Differences between model and Glasgow
Concentric		
Sector		
Multiple nuclei		

Fig. 84

New Towns

All the villages and towns studied so far have grown up in stages — each new piece being planned, then built depending on where and when conditions permit. A **New Town** however is a **planned** town whose general structure was agreed upon before any building took place.

Why were they built?

There were two main reasons:
1. To provide homes for the people being moved out of the older decaying towns of Central Scotland which were undergoing **urban renewal.**
2. To encourage new industry into Central Scotland and so provide work for those people made redundant due to the decline of the old **heavy** industries.

For each New Town a **Development Corporation** was given the authority to plan and co-ordinate the construction of the New Town and to make sure the mistakes made in the **old** towns, due to lack of overall planning, were not repeated.

Where were they built?

Five New Towns have been built so far in East Kilbride, Glenrothes, Cumbernauld, Livingston and Irvine. All lie in the Central lowlands near to the older towns and cities from where they have drawn their population (see Fig. 44). As a result the people of the New Towns have not been drawn too far away from their families and friends.

The structure of a New Town

Each New Town was planned so that it would be **self-contained** i.e. the people housed there could also work and enjoy all other aspects of life without having to leave its boundaries. As a result certain land use features are found in most of the New Towns. These features are shown in Fig. 85.

The town centre

In the centre of the New Town is an area of offices, shops and other services e.g. a cinema, banks, a large leisure centre and police station — all services which need to be easily reached and so are in the centre.

Here are found some of the shops which need to be visited only occasionally e.g. shoe shops, clothes shops, jewellery shops and large supermarkets visited weekly for bulk buying of the week's food supply.

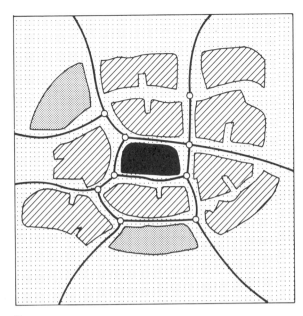

Key

■	Town centre	▨	Industrial estates
▨	Neighbourhoods	⋮	'Green areas'
O	Roundabout	—	Main road (dual carriageway)

Fig. 85   Model of a New Town

New Town centres have **pedestrian precincts** i.e. areas where only supply vehicles for the shops or emergency vehicles like an ambulance are allowed to disturb the pedestrians. Parts of the shopping centre may be covered (see Fig. 86) and heated creating 'all weather shopping conditions'.

Neighbourhoods

These are the residential areas of the New Towns. Unlike many housing estates in the **older** towns Neighbourhoods contain many amenities needed by the population living there e.g. most have schools (which may open at night for academic and leisure activities), a shopping centre where 'everyday' goods can be bought (see Fig. 87), a library, a church, a community centre and play areas for children. The houses may be a mixture of designs sizes and shapes to attract different types of people, thereby balancing the population.

Fig. 87   Ladywell shopping centre, Livingston

Industrial estates

To encourage industry into the New Towns large **industrial estates** (see Fig. 88) have been built with several attractive features for the industrialist:
(a) The Government provide high cash grants e.g. for building factories and buying machinery for industrialists willing to locate in New Towns.
(b) They are well served by communications — especially by roads and most have close

Fig. 86   Shopping mall in Irvine

61

Fig. 88   Industrial estate, Livingston

links with large ports or airports so movement of materials can be carried out efficiently.

(c) There are usually large markets nearby where products can be sold e.g. Glasgow and Edinburgh.

(d) They are usually pleasantly **landscaped** with the factories already built and serviced with electricity and water — firms can build their own factories on the estate if they wish. Such industrial estates are usually separated from the neighbourhood and most are on the edges of the New Towns so that heavy lorries transporting goods can get in and out of the town easily. This also reduces traffic near the town centre and pollution caused by exhaust fumes.

Unlike those in the older towns the industries attracted to the New Towns are mainly **light** industries i.e. they produce lightweight goods, dependent much more on **road** transport than railways or canals. They are **diversified** i.e. there are many types and most are **mobile** i.e. they can move around since they are not dependent on one particular location. For example the fact that they are powered by electricity allows them to select a location well away from coalfields.

Green belts

So that the 'continuous urban sprawl' common among older towns is not allowed to develop, most New Towns are surrounded by **green belts** (areas of countryside where the building of factories and houses is forbidden) and the neighbourhoods, industrial estates and shopping centre are separated by 'landscaped' areas of trees, grass or shrubs. These green areas allow recreation, many having leisure walks, football parks and tennis courts.

Communications

Movement into and within the town mainly depends on **road** transport. For the most efficient movement of traffic several **dual carriageways** (double roads) have been built to allow fast movement through or from one part of the town to another. The dual carriageways usually converge on **roundabouts** from which **access** roads lead into car parks or cul-de-sacs in the town centre, neighbourhoods or industrial estates (see Fig. 88). Since these access roads are usually much narrower and winding, the traffic is slowed down, making the industrial estates and neighbourhoods safer for pedestrians. People need never cross the main roads since underpasses and overpasses are provided.

For those without cars **community routes** are provided i.e. roads on which only buses are allowed. These people can therefore be transported around the New Town as efficiently as possible.

Exercise

1 (a) Explain the difference between an expanding **Old Town** and a **New Town**. *1 mark*
(b) Give two reasons why the development of New Towns was necessary. *2 marks*
(c) Name the New Towns of Scotland. *1 mark*

2 Examine O.S. Map 5 and the land-use map of East Kilbride (Fig. 89).
(a) Name Industrial Estates, A, C, and D. (B = Nerston). *1½ marks*
(b) Three of these estates are on the outskirts of the town. Give two advantages of such a location — one for the industries and one for the people of the town. *2 marks*
(c) Choose the three words from the following list which best describe the industries likely to be found on such estates:

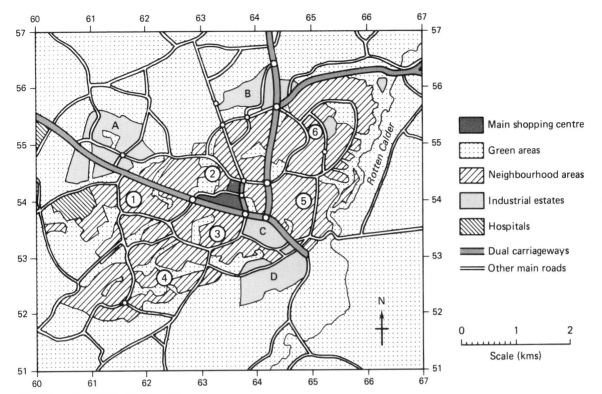

Fig. 89   East Kilbride New Town

heavy; light; mobile; declining; diversified; integrated. *3 marks*

(d) Explain the meaning of the three words you have chosen. *3 marks*

(e) List four reasons why industries have been attracted to New Towns. *4 marks*

(f) Name the form of power and form of transport these industries are most likely to use. *2 marks*

3 (a) Look at Fig. 89. Name neighbourhoods 1–6 (2 is shown in two parts on the map extract). *3 marks*

(b) List some of the features which make neighbourhoods different from ordinary housing estates. *3 marks*

4 (a) Look at Fig. 89. Explain why the main shopping centre is located in the centre of the town. *1 mark*

(b) Suggest two ways in which the shops in this centre are different from those in the neighbourhoods. *2 marks*

(c) This shopping centre takes the form of a **pedestrian precinct.** Explain this term. *1 mark*

5 Explain why it is highly unlikely that there will be any urban growth in the area between East Kilbride and Glasgow e.g. in square 6256. *1 mark*

6 (a) Explain why the railway running north-eastwards from East Kilbride (square 6556) should

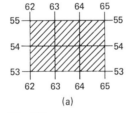
(a)

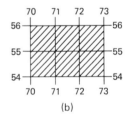
(b)

Fig. 90

have been closed in such a rapidly growing area of housing and industry. *1 mark*

(b) Refer to the map extract and count the number of **roundabouts** within the areas shown in Fig. 90(a) and (b) — **Note:** the areas are of equal size but they are not to the correct scale. *1 mark*

(c) Try to explain your answer referring to the structure of New Towns. *1 mark*

(d) What is meant by a cul-de-sac? *½ mark*

(e) Why are they thought to be so important in New Towns? *1 mark*

7 Imagine that for the first 13 years of your life you lived in an old part of Glasgow, near the city centre, then moved to a New Town. You have now lived there for over one year. Write an account in at least 150 words describing how your life in the New Town would be different from that in Glasgow. *5 marks*

Total 40 marks

63

The growth of towns — the shrinking of the countryside

The shrinking countryside

Scottish towns and cities have grown at an incredible rate in the last 200 years and, as the pie charts in Fig. 91 indicate, Scotland has changed from being mainly **rural** (where its population lives mainly in villages and farms) to mainly **urban** (where its population lives mainly in towns and cities).

It has become obvious that the towns and cities of Scotland are gradually 'swallowing up' the countryside as they grow and that unless careful planning is carried out much of Scotland's naturally beautiful countryside is going to disappear in a mass of 'urban sprawl'. It is important that this is never allowed to happen since the countryside has several important functions:
(a) land is used for farming and forestry;
(b) it is a home for millions of plants and animals;
(c) it is an important recreational source for people.

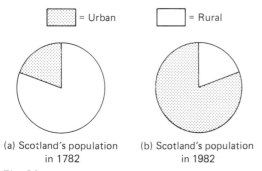

= Urban   = Rural

(a) Scotland's population in 1782   (b) Scotland's population in 1982

Fig. 91

Protecting the countryside against development, i.e. **conservation**

Today, local authorities are well aware of how important the countryside is to the population. When development plans are introduced certain areas are identified where urban development needs encouragement and other areas where it needs to be discouraged. This ensures that land is used in the most appropriate way possible. This is not such an easy task as it sounds since different people have different ideas on how the land should best be used. **Land use conflicts** often arise between people competing for the use of an area of land e.g. farmers are unlikely to agree that an area of flat fertile land would best be used for an industrial development such as the one shown in Fig. 92.

Several important methods of safeguarding or **conserving** particularly valuable areas against certain types of development have been devised.

1. **Green Belts** — these have been introduced around many of Scotland's old towns as well as New Towns.

2. **Conservation Areas** — in many rural areas some villages have buildings of distinctive character and architectural interest. Such villages may be declared Conservation Areas in which all new buildings or modernisation must be carefully designed to blend in with the area's existing character.

3. **National Nature Reserves** — these are stretches of land looked after by the **Nature Conservancy Council**, which contain valuable types of wildlife habitats or important natural physical features.

4. **National Scenic Areas** (see Fig. 93) — these are areas of outstanding scenery which the **Countryside Commission for Scotland** feel should be protected against certain types of development. The Commission must be consulted before any project which may significantly affect the scenery in these areas takes place.

These are not the only areas where the landscape and wildlife is conserved. Before any development can take place today the developer must convince the local authorities that their buildings will cause the minimum damage possible to the landscape. Many buildings must now be 'landscaped' or 'screened' by trees, bushes shrubs and grassed areas to hide them from the public eye and provide homes for wildlife. In addition there are laws to protect birds and other wildlife in many parts of the country e.g. there are 'close seasons' when it is against the law to

Fig. 92   Building an industrial estate

Fig. 93   Scotland's Country Parks and National
Scenic Areas

hunt for game animals.

Despite all these measures the survival of the countryside depends mainly on whether those who manage the land e.g. farmers and other landowners, consider conservation to be important and whether the general public make sure The Country Code is followed.

Countryside and recreation

During the last fifty years more people have visited the countryside. Mobility has increased with more widespread car ownership and people have more free time. They are attracted to the countryside by its scenery, the freedom it provides to enjoy outdoor activities, the chance to study wildlife, visit places of interest, enjoy its peace and quiet and get away from the everyday pressures of town and city life. As a result there has been an increase in the demand for places in the countryside where people can enjoy outdoor activities. In response to this demand and concern about rural development the **Countryside Commission for Scotland** was set up to help in the conservation and improvement of the countryside and to help planning authorities

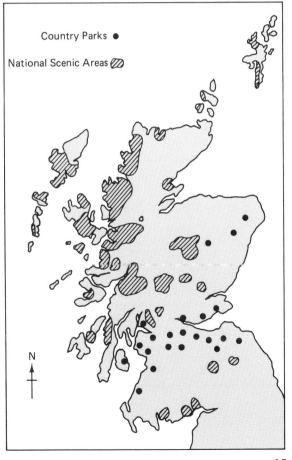

Country Parks ●

National Scenic Areas

N

provide facilities for people to enjoy it. With these aims in mind the Commission has provided large grants to help planning authorities develop a wide range of recreational facilities (viewpoints footpaths and trails, youth hostels and car parks) throughout Scotland and several Country Parks have been set up (Fig. 93).

These **Country Parks** are areas of countryside usually near to a town or city, where people go and relax and enjoy countryside activities. They are much larger and contain different facilities from **Urban Parks** i.e. parks within a city or town (see Figs. 94 and 95). They all have a **ranger service** to supply the public with advice on where to go and what to do. Most have picnic areas and many have nature trails and visitor centres designed to stimulate interest in the area and generally increase enjoyment.

More recently, there have been plans to set up much larger **Regional Parks** (such as that near Renfrew), where recreation will be an important consideration but much more of the land will be used for other purposes like farming and forestry.

The Countryside Commission is not the only organisation providing 'places for people' in the countryside e.g. **The Forestry Commission** have recreational facilities in their forest parks while the **National Trust for Scotland**, which looks after large areas of the country, including islands, waterfalls, lochs and mountains provides facilities for visitors.

Exercise

1 Write a paragraph of at least 100 words explaining why many people think 'the countryside must never be allowed to disappear under urban development'.

2 Explain the meaning of the following terms: **recreation; National Nature Reserve; conservation; open season.**

3 Suggest which groups of people may be involved in **land use conflicts** in Fig. 92.

4 The following are the rules included in the new 'Country Code'. Select five of these rules and explain why each is important.

Enjoy the countryside and respect its life and work
Guard against all risk of fire
Fasten all gates
Keep your dogs under close control
Keep to public paths across farmland
Use gates and stiles to cross fences, hedges and walls
Leave livestock, crops and machinery alone
Take your litter home
Help to keep all water clean
Protect wildlife, plants and trees
Take special care on country roads
Make no unnecessary noise

5 Give two reasons why the need for recreational facilities in the countryside has increased in the last few years.

6 Look at Fig. 93.
(a) Describe and explain the distribution of **Country Parks** in Scotland.
(b) The map also shows the **National Scenic Areas** in Scotland.
   (i) Explain what is meant by a National Scenic Area;
   (ii) Describe the scenery you would expect to find in some of these areas (Fig. 1 on p. 4 may help you to answer this question).

7 Look carefully at Figs. 94 and 95. Describe the major differences between the two parks. Your answer should refer to size, location, functions and facilities.

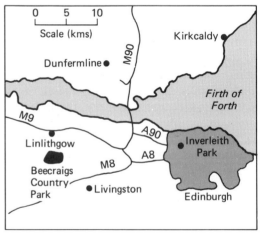

Fig. 94   Location of an Urban Park and Country Park in Lothian region

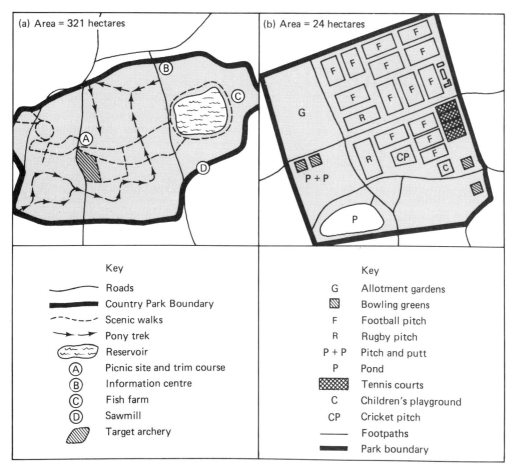

(a) Area = 321 hectares

(b) Area = 24 hectares

Key

— Roads
━━ Country Park Boundary
- - - Scenic walks
→ Pony trek
〜 Reservoir
Ⓐ Picnic site and trim course
Ⓑ Information centre
Ⓒ Fish farm
Ⓓ Sawmill
▨ Target archery

Key

G   Allotment gardens
▨   Bowling greens
F   Football pitch
R   Rugby pitch
P + P   Pitch and putt
P   Pond
▨   Tennis courts
C   Children's playground
CP   Cricket pitch
——   Footpaths
━━   Park boundary

Fig. 95 a)   Beecraigs Country Park   Fig. 95 b)   Inverleith Park (Urban Park in Edinburgh)

5

Industry in Central Scotland

The location of manufacturing industries

Many considerations have to be taken into account when building a factory. Site is an extremely important one as a factory cannot be built anywhere. There are a group of **locational factors** which the industrialist must consider when deciding where to locate a factory. These are shown in Fig. 96. Each factor shown in the boxes tends to 'pull' the industry in a certain direction.

Power supply
Industrial machines must be powered. In the past many different sources of power have been used, e.g. wind, water, coal and oil, and since these are costly (or impossible) to transport, the industrial works tended to be located near to the sources of power e.g. near a river or on a coalfield. During the Industrial Revolution i.e. the period around 1760–1830 when Scotland's industry grew at its greatest rate, **coal** was by far the most important source of heat and power. Most of Scotland's large industrial towns and cities therefore are located on or near coalfields. Nowadays, however, running water, coal and oil can be converted into **electricity** (the main source of power) in large power stations and since electricity can be transported very easily by transmission lines, the factories are not usually 'pulled' so much towards the original sources of power — they are more **mobile**. Cheap electricity rates can however be used by an electricity board to encourage an industry into a particular area.

Labour (workers)
All industries need workers. Some require a great deal of expertise; others require workers with particular skills, while others need a variety of workers. Most industries are therefore attracted to large centres of population where labour is plentiful or to areas where people have particular skills or expertise.

Market
An industry's **market** consists of anyone wishing to buy its products at a price which enables the industrialist to make a profit. It costs money to transport products so the nearer the factory to its market(s) the better. If the factory's products are bulkier, more fragile or more perishable than its raw materials then a location near the market is particularly attractive.

Raw materials
Every factory needs materials from which to manufacture products. These materials can be taken from many sources e.g. the ground, the sea, or other factories. An ironworks obtains the raw iron from the ground, a car manufacturer obtains steel from a steelworks, glass from a glassworks, etc. Again these materials are expensive to transport, and so the industry is 'pulled' towards their source.

Site
An industry's site is the actual piece of land the factory lies on. The site is vitally important since the land must be fairly flat for building on and stable to support the buildings like factories and works.

Transport facilities
The labour and raw materials must be transported to the factory and the finished

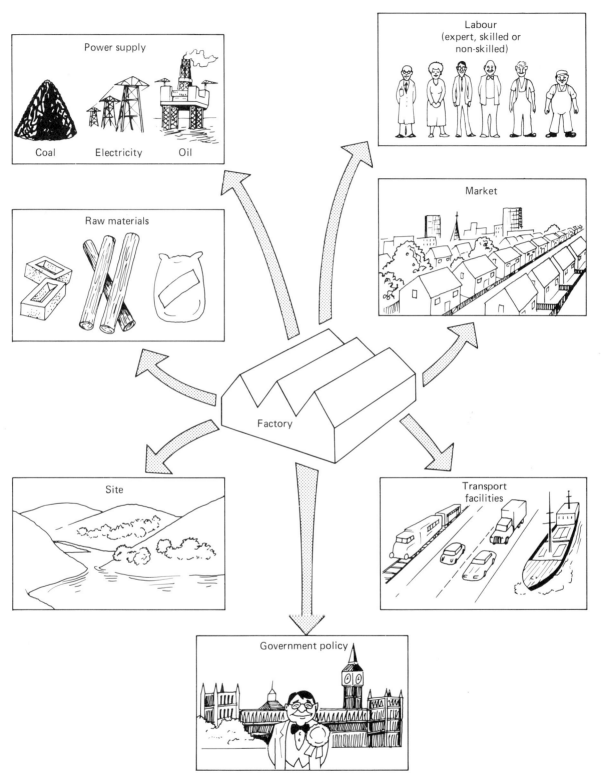

Fig. 96

products must be transported from the factory to the market. If the rail-links, sea-links and (especially nowadays) road-links are poor in an area then not only will goods be difficult to transport but they will cost more. Little industry will be encouraged in such an area.

Government policy

The government offers incentives (like grants and loans for building factories or buying machinery) to industrialists willing to locate a factory in areas hardest hit by unemployment or population loss. These incentives are often very attractive to industrialists.

Every industrialist must consider each of these seven factors when deciding where to locate a factory or works. In many cases one locational factor tends to have a greater pull than the others. This depends on the type of products being manufactured in the factory. For example, a knitwear factory powered by electricity does not need a huge area of flat land, wool and other raw materials can be transported easily as can the finished clothes, but a large number of fairly skilled workers are needed. In this case the labour supply is the most important factor.

Exercise

1 Each of the following industries is dominated by one particular locational factor. Choosing your answers from the following, **labour**, **power supply**, **market**, **raw materials**, decide which factor dominates in each case, and give reasons for each answer.
  (a) Bakery
  (b) Creamery
  (c) Aluminium smelter (requires great amounts of electrical energy to smelt the metal)
  (d) Computer manufacturer

The old heavy industries of Central Scotland

The growth of many of the large towns in Central Scotland was greatly encouraged by the development of **heavy** industries. We shall now look at two such industries in detail, **coal mining** and **iron and steelmaking**.

Coal mining in Scotland

Coal is a sedimentary rock formed from the remains of plants which grew in lowland swamps millions of years ago. When these plants died the damp conditions prevented them decaying completely. Their remains were slowly covered by many layers of rock brought down from surrounding upland areas by rivers. The enormous weight of these overlying rocks gradually changed the dead plant material into a 'black rock which burns'.

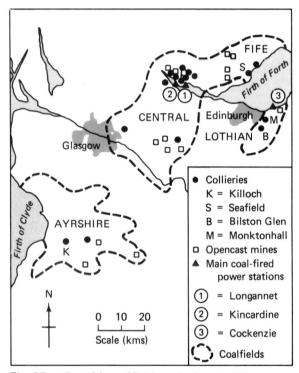

Fig. 97   Scottish coalfields and mines, 1983

The growth of coal mining

Coal has been mined in Scotland since the Middle Ages when monks used it for heating their abbeys. Mines in the early days were very simple affairs extracting coal where the seams reached the surface i.e. from the **exposed coalfields**. Many were 'opencast' mines where any covering layer of soil or rock was removed before the coal was extracted or 'adit' mines where shallow tunnels were dug into coal seams which were exposed along valleys (see

Fig. 102). Coal output remained low however until the late 18th century. The new inventions of the **Industrial Revolution** not only allowed coal to be mined from much deeper seams but also opened up many new uses for it in addition to its role in heating buildings, e.g. producing steam to drive factory machinery, ships and locomotives, smelting iron ore, and producing gas and other chemicals.

In the 19th century the demand for Scottish coal increased rapidly both at home and abroad and a **large number** of **small** mines opened up in Central Scotland. Industries like iron and steel, shipbuilding, engineering, chemicals and textiles sprung up in settlements lying on the coalfields or at railway or port locations where coal could be brought in efficiently.

Most of Scotland's largest towns and cities experienced their most rapid growth at this time as people flocked from the countryside looking for work in these industries.

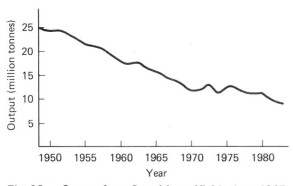

Fig. 98   Output from Scottish coalfields since 1947

Exercise

1 Examine Fig. 97 and answer the following questions:
(a) In which of Scotland's three main physical sections do the coalfields lie?
(b) Compare the map of Scotland's population distribution (Fig. 6 on p. 9) with Fig. 97.
(i) Can you see any similarity between the coalfield areas and the most densely populated areas of Scotland?
(ii) Explain your answer.

The decline of coal-mining

Since the peak in production in 1913, there has been a gradual **decline** in output from Scottish coalfields. There are several reasons for this, including:

1. The coal seams which were exposed and nearest the surface were first to be mined, and as a result, the coal in these seams was gradually used up. The deeper seams must now be mined and this has resulted in great expense for the industry.

2. Many of the seams left are badly faulted, folded or very thin, making them difficult and expensive to mine.

3. The **demand** for coal began to fall as other cheaper 'cleaner' sources of power and fuel became available e.g. **oil** (firstly from foreign states such as those in the Middle East, then more recently from the North Sea) and **natural gas** (also from the North Sea). These are now being used to heat many homes and factories, to produce electricity in power stations, and in rail transport the diesel oil and electric engines have replaced the steam engine.

Fig. 99

The National Coal Board
In 1947 the government took over most of the mines in this country i.e. they **nationalised** them and placed them under the National Coal Board. The N.C.B. has taken several steps to make the coal industry more competitive:

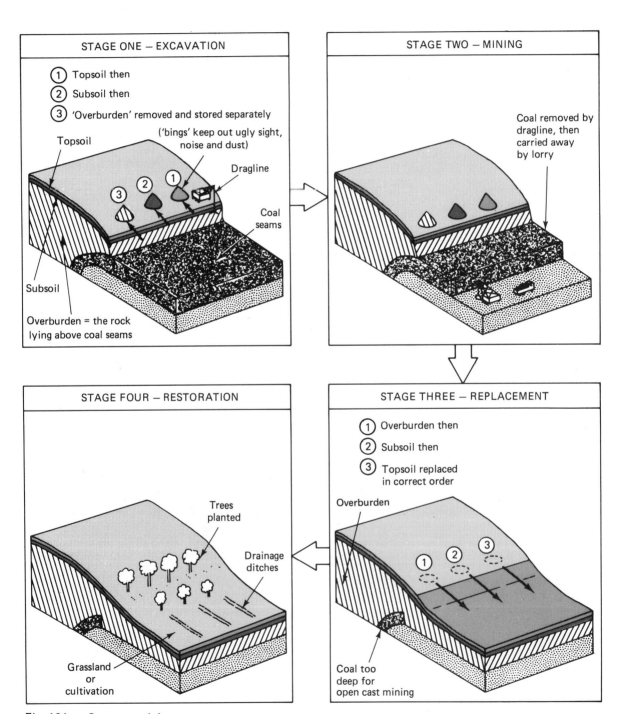

STAGE ONE — EXCAVATION

① Topsoil then

② Subsoil then

③ 'Overburden' removed and stored separately

('bings' keep out ugly sight, noise and dust)

Topsoil

Dragline

③ ② ①

Coal seams

Subsoil

Overburden = the rock lying above coal seams

STAGE TWO — MINING

Coal removed by dragline, then carried away by lorry

STAGE THREE — REPLACEMENT

① Overburden then

② Subsoil then

③ Topsoil replaced in correct order

Overburden

① ② ③

Coal too deep for open cast mining

STAGE FOUR — RESTORATION

Trees planted

Drainage ditches

Grassland or cultivation

Fig. 101   Opencast mining

72

1. Many pits considered least likely to make a profit (i.e. the smaller pits or those with poorer seams) have been closed down and production has been concentrated in a small number of large, deep, new (or modernised) collieries. In 1947 there were 187 N.C.B. collieries in Scotland. By 1982 this had been reduced to 16.

2. Millions of pounds have been spent on new machinery (see Fig. 99), techniques and exploration for new coal seams.

3. Some mines have been linked by underground tunnels to form larger more efficient units e.g. Solsgirth, Castlehill and Bogside mines lying north of the Firth of Forth have been linked by an 8.8 km tunnel. Coal from each mine is carried through the tunnel by a conveyor belt to Longannet mine where it is crushed, checked for quality then carried to the nearby Longannet Power Station (Fig. 100). This whole process is controlled by a large computer.

Fig. 100   Longannet power station

4. 'Opencast' mining has been re-developed. Although this was one of the earliest forms of coal mining, only very small amounts of coal could be extracted by this method. Nowadays however, with huge draglines (see Fig. 105 on p. 75) seams up to 200 metres deep can be excavated. Fig. 101 illustrates the processes involved in 'opencast' mining.

The main disadvantage of these changes has been that they have led to an increase in local unemployment figures. Whereas in 1947 the N.C.B. employed 81 000 miners in Scotland, today the figure is less than 20 000. The changes have however made the British coal industry more efficient and as a result of this and the huge increases in the price of oil in 1974 and 1979 coal is now cheaper than oil in this country. On the other hand North Sea Gas and nuclear energy are cheaper still and both have captured markets from coal in recent years.

Exercise

1 Examine the three models in Fig. 102 showing a typical Scottish coalfield at different times in history and answer the questions below.
   (a) Describe the changes on the coalfield
      (i) from 1750 to 1913
      (ii) since 1913.
   Your answer should refer to the **number, depth** and **size** of **mines**.
   (b) Describe and give reasons for the trend shown on Fig. 98.
   (c) List four measures taken by the National Coal Board to make the coal industry more efficient.

2 Explain the difference between an **exposed** and a **concealed** coalfield.

3 Examine the pie chart (Fig. 103).
   (a) What is the main market for Scotland's coal?
   (b) Approximately what proportion of Scotland's coal does this market use?
   (c) Describe the effect this use of coal has on the **distribution** of **modern** industry in Scotland.

4 Examine O.S. Map 4 and Fig. 104 showing the collleries in the Cumnock area in 1953 and 1983.
   (a) Find three of the four mines open in 1953 which lay along the Southern Boundary Fault and give six-figure grid references for their location.
   (b) Suggest the most likely reasons why these mines have closed down.
   (c) There are now no mines worked in the Airds Moss area north of Cumnock which at one time was covered in small mines. Write down as many pieces of map evidence you can find to confirm this statement.

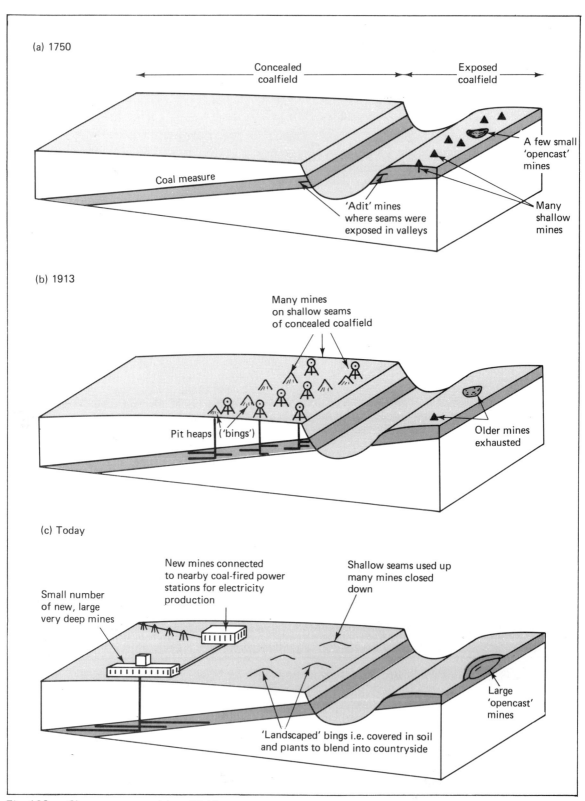

Fig. 102   Changes on a model coalfield

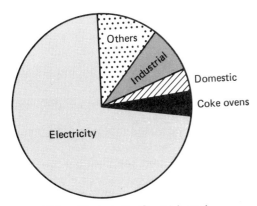

Fig. 103   Markets for Scottish coal

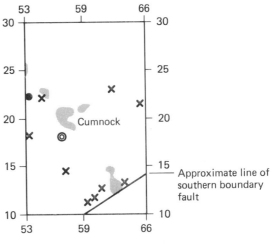

- ● Mine open 1983 (Barony)
- ✗ Mines open in 1953 but closed in 1983
- ◎ Opencast mine (Bowes)

Fig. 104

5 Examine the photographs (Figs. 105 and 106) showing an opencast mining area such as that found south of Cumnock during and after mining operations.

(a) Explain what is meant by an **opencast** mine;

(b) Explain why large-scale opencast mining is only a relatively recent development;

(c) Describe the steps which must be taken to restore the natural beauty of an area affected by opencast mining;

(d) Suggest why the overburden subsoil and topsoil must be replaced in a particular order;

(e) If coal is to be mined by the opencast method there are often protests from local people, while others in the area may welcome such developments. Explain these two different attitudes.

The Scottish iron and steel industry

Think of as many things as you can which are made of iron or steel, and list them in your jotter. This list will illustrate the importance of iron (and especially) steel to our society today.

Steel is a substance made up of iron and a very small amount of carbon. It is much stronger and harder than iron, so most of the iron coming into Scotland today is used to make steel.

Fig. 105

Fig. 106

75

Making steel

Fig. 107 shows some of the main processes involved in making steel today.

Note:

1. The 'customers' for the steel strip or slabs may be other steelworks where the steel is rolled into sheets or plate before being sold to steel-using industries all over the country.

2. In the past the ironworks and steelworks were often separate but now they are increasingly found together in **integrated steelworks**. This reduces transport costs and makes the production of steel more efficient.

Iron and steel making in Scotland

The iron industry developed in the 18th century in Central Scotland since all three raw materials i.e. iron ore, limestone and charcoal (for providing heat to melt iron) were found fairly close together in this area. Even when coal became the main source of heat for blast furnaces Central Scotland was again fortunate in having plentiful supplies of coking coal. As a result **many, small scattered** ironworks developed. With the onset of the Industrial Revolution there was a huge demand for iron and (later) steel, from within Central Scotland itself (from the shipbuilding, engineering, textile and construction industries) and later from abroad. The iron and steel industry therefore flourished for a long time on or near the coalfields of Central Scotland.

Since then however the industry has been affected by several problems. **Iron ore** deposits have been exhausted and home coal has become much more expensive. As a result all of the ore and much of the coal needed by Scottish steelworks has to be imported at great expense. Many of the traditional steel-using industries have declined and so new markets have had to be found. Lighter steel products have become much more important and the industry has had to face increasing competition from steelworks in other countries e.g. Japan, West Germany, U.S.A. Steel production continued to rise however for much of this century.

British Steel Corporation

In 1967, the government nationalised most of the steelworks in this country and placed them under the British Steel Corporation. The B.S.C. like the N.C.B. has carried out several measures aimed at making their industry more competitive. The small, out-of-date iron and steelworks which were losing most money have been closed down while other works have been modernised e.g. by the replacement of old hand-fed blast furnaces by new mechanically fed ones, the installation of new steel furnaces and the development of the **continuous casting** process (see Fig. 107). This latter process converts molten steel **directly** into solid slabs without having to pass through other stages first. Ideally, in a steelworks the raw ore should go in at one end and pass out at the other end as usable steel in a continuous process. In the past metal had to be cooled and reheated as it moved from one stage to another but with the modernisation of steelworks the ideal situation is getting closer all the time.

Such changes have brought similar benefits and problems to those made by the N.C.B. i.e. the industry is now more efficient but there are fewer jobs for steelworkers.

Recent problems

Despite their increased efficiency Scottish steelworks have found it very difficult to sell their steel in recent years. There has been a worldwide **recession** i.e. a drop in trade since 1974 and world demand for steel has stopped growing.

Furthermore many countries which used to import British steel now produce (and export) their own.

Home markets have also shrunk. One of the main customers for Scottish steel — the car factory at Linwood — closed in 1981 and the recession has forced many other steel-using industries to close down or cut back on production. As a result the B.S.C. has closed down a large number of steelworks in Central Scotland (and elsewhere in the U.K.) and steel production has been reduced.

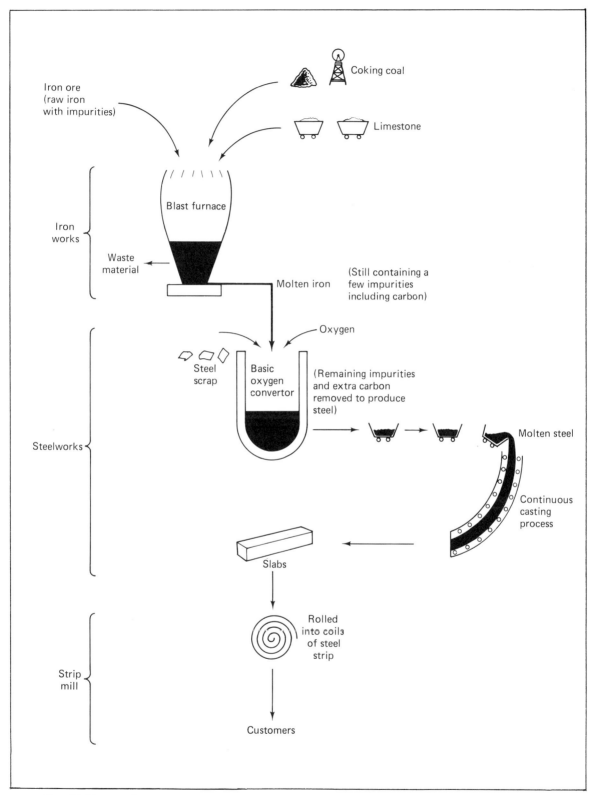

Fig. 107   Making steel

Exercise

1 Examine Fig. 107 carefully and describe the part played by (a) The Blast Furnace; (b) The Basic Oxygen Converter; (c) The Strip Mill, in producing steel ready for sale to customers.

2 Explain:
(a) Why Central Scotland was an ideal location for the development of the iron and steel industry in the 19th century;
(b) Why this location is no longer ideal.

3 Examine Fig. 108.
(a) Describe the **distribution** of British Steel works in Scotland in 1983.
(b) How has the **number** of works in this area changed since 1974?
(c) Explain your answer to (b).
(d) How has this change affected unemployment figures in Central Scotland?

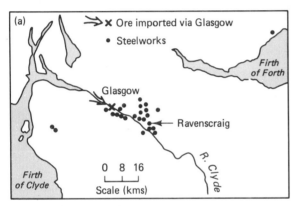

Fig. 108 a)   British Steel works in Scotland 1974

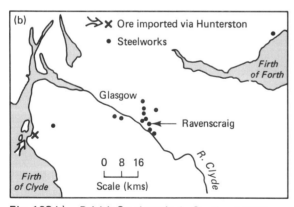

Fig. 108 b)   British Steel works in Scotland 1983

Industrial inertia (geographical inertia)

Central Scotland no longer provides an ideal location for the steel industry. All of the iron ore and much of the coal has to be imported. The markets for the steel have diminished greatly and several of the works are losing great amounts of money — yet the industry remains here. This situation is called **industrial inertia**. Why does the B.S.C. not close down **all** those works making a loss? The reason for this is that their removal could be disastrous to areas like Central Scotland. As well as the jobs in the steelworks themselves being lost, other industries using the steel produced would all be faced with increased costs of obtaining raw materials and they might in turn be forced to close down. Unemployment levels would rise still further, the standard of living of the local people would drop and many would be forced to leave the area altogether. British governments have therefore pumped large amounts of money into the industry so that the most efficient works are kept open.

Ravenscraig Steelworks in Motherwell

Of the 11 000 people employed in the iron and steel industry in Scotland 4500 are employed at **Ravenscraig Steelworks** — a huge works completed in 1963 (see Fig. 109).

Ravenscraig is an **integrated** steelworks i.e. it has ironworks and steelworks (as well as a stripmill) combined on the same site and all the processes illustrated in Fig. 107 are carried out there. Today much of the coal and all of the iron ore required by this huge complex is imported via a large deep water terminal at Hunterston on the Firth of Clyde (see Fig. 163, p. 117) and transported to Ravenscraig by rail.

Much of the steel made here is transported by rail to smaller works in Central Scotland where it is rolled into sheets or plates and sold to customers throughout the country, e.g. the truck manufacturers at **Bathgate**, the **Hoover** Domestic Appliance manufacturers at Cambuslang and the car manufacturers in the English Midlands.

Fig. 109   Ravenscraig Steelworks: A Strip mill B Steelworks C Blast furnaces D Cooling towers E Double
track railway F Mineral railway line G Motherwell town centre H Flat, green area

Other steelworks in Scotland
These tend to have specialised equipment for the production of specialised steel products (i.e. products made for one specific purpose) like pipes for North Sea oil production.

Excrcise

1 Fig. 110 shows part of the continuous casting process in Ravenscraig Steelworks.
    (a) Explain what is happening in this process.
    (b) Explain why it is so important to steelmaking today.

2 (a) What term is used to describe a situation where an industry remains in an area despite the fact that the original reasons for it being there have disappeared?
    (b) Explain why Ravenscraig works has been kept open despite massive losses.

Fig. 110

79

3 Examine Fig. 109 and O.S. Map 5. The steelworks can be found in the shaded area shown in Fig. 111.

(a) Using map evidence and the labels on Fig. 109 state the direction in whcih the camera was facing when the photograph was taken.

(b) Using map evidence explain why Ravenscraig was a suitable site for a steelworks.

(c) What structures do the small pink circles on the map represent?

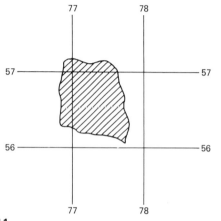

Fig. 111

Fig. 112

Old and new industrial landscapes

Old industrial landscapes

Coal has not only influenced the **location** of industry but also the **landscapes** which have developed. Due to the importance of coal to industry and the rapid growth in industrial development a certain type of landscape resulted. This old industrial landscape developed in most of the large towns and cities in Central Scotland. Such an old type landscape is shown in Fig. 112.

These landscapes can be found in most large towns and cities although many coalmines have now closed down or been filled in. Often the bings (waste-heaps) have been removed or landscaped but many of the old factories and houses still remain in the towns while in other areas they too may have undergone urban renewal or have been knocked down to leave patches of land for new development. Figs. 113 and 114 illustrate some typical old industrial landscapes.

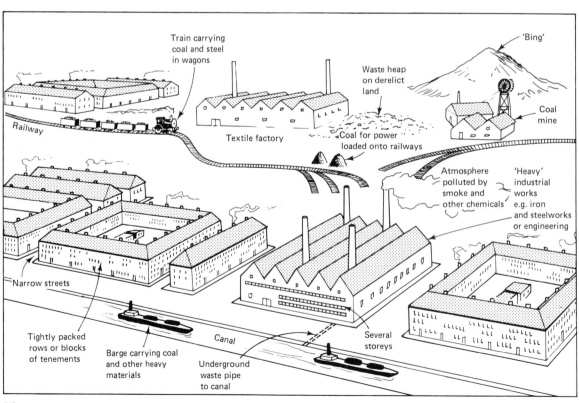

Exercise

Examine Figs. 113 and 114 and list the features on each which show evidence of **old** industrial landscapes.

New industrial landscapes

Not all industrial landscapes look like those in Figs. 113 and 114 however. A **new industrial**

Fig. 113   An old industrial landscape in Falkirk

Fig. 114   An old industrial landscape in Dundee

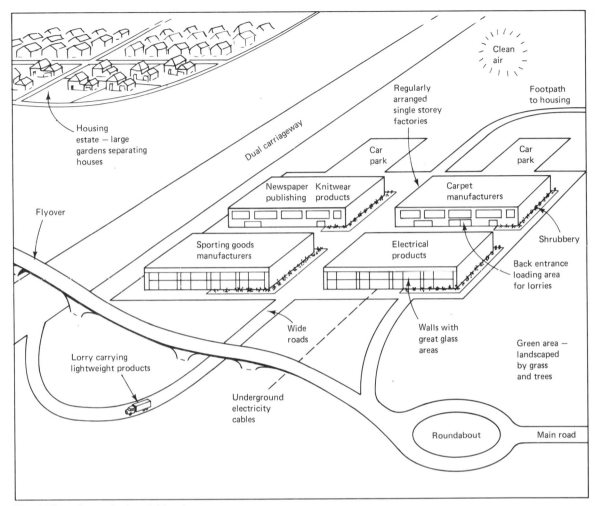

Fig. 115   A new industrial landscape

landscape looks entirely different. It has some of the features shown in Fig. 115. Such new industrial landscapes have gradually developed in the 20th century due to two main changes:
1. The development of power stations which can produce **electricity** — a form of energy which can be transported easily along wires and can be used to produce heat and power machinery. Industries are therefore no longer restricted to coalfields and no longer need huge chimneys to lead the smoke from burning coal into the atmosphere.
2. The development of **road** transport like buses, lorries and motor cars. Now people need not live as close to their work and industrial estates can be built well away from homes on main roads on the outskirts of towns and cities. Here much more space is

available and land is cheaper.

These new industrial landscapes are much more carefully planned and laid out so that the problems of overcrowding, congestion and pollution found on the old industrial landscapes do not occur here.

Exercise

1 Examine Fig. 116 which shows an industrial estate in Edinburgh.
   (a) State whether this is an old or a new industrial landscape.
   (b) Give at least four pieces of evidence from the photograph to support your answer.

2 (a) List three ways in which the environment around new estates is more pleasant than that in old industrial areas.

82

Fig. 116   An industrial estate in Edinburgh

(b) Explain why new industrial estates:
  (i) need not be near any coalfield;
  (ii) need not be intermingled with housing;
  (iii) can be spread out over a large area.

3 Copy and complete the table Fig. 117 using the words or phrases below.

A near town centre / on outskirts of town;
B near to factories / far from factories;
C cramped together along narrow streets / well spread out;
D single storey / two or more storey;
E cramped irregularly together / well spaced out;
F small and few in number / cover large area;
G well landscaped with grass and shrubs in regular rows / derelict and covered in waste materials;
H mainly roads / mainly canals and railways;
I large parking space / little or no car parks;
J very small if they exist / very tall;
K polluted with smoke and other waste / clean air and rivers;

L light and heavyweight / mainly lightweight;
M many different types / few types;
N originally coal but now electricity / always has been electricity.

Government aid to industry

Many of Scotland's older industries e.g. coal mining and shipbuilding have undergone a long decline since the early years of this century. The new industries which have grown up this century have been attracted much more to other parts of Britain, particularly to the big markets of S.E. England.

    An examination of Fig. 118 starting with 'Decrease in number of industries' shows how this has affected many areas in Scotland. Notice that one change can lead directly to

83

Feature	'Old' industrial landscape	'New' industrial landscape
A Location of factories		
B Location of housing		
C Arrangement of housing		
D Height of factories		
E Arrangement of factories		
F Factory windows		
G Land surrounding factories		
H Main form of communication		
I Size of car parks		
J Chimneys on houses and factories		
K Air and rivers		
L Type of product from industry		
M Number of products from industry		
N Power source for factories		

Fig. 117   Old and new industrial landscapes — a comparison

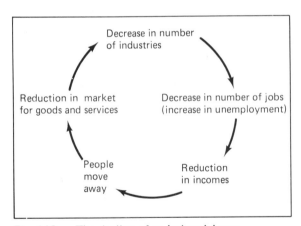

Fig. 118   The decline of an industrial area

another and that unless something is done to break one of the links the problem becomes worse and worse.

Since the 1930s British governments have taken various steps to try and break these 'cycles' and bring employment, wealth and people back to such areas:

1. Incentives have been offered to firms willing to set up in areas hit hardest by unemployment and population loss. These incentives have mainly been in the form of fixed-rate cash grants for building factories and buying machinery but in many cases there are extra job-related grants available.

There are three categories of areas entitled to assistance (see Fig. 119).

(i) 'Special Development Areas' with the most severe problems — industries are entitled to fixed-rate grants at 22% for new factories and machinery. The extra job-related assistance is available in addition.

Note: the New Towns are also considered as Special Development Areas in order to encourage the growth of industry within them.

(ii) 'Development Areas' also with great problems — industries are entitled to fixed-rate grants at 15% and, again the extra job-related assistance may also be available.

(iii) 'Intermediate Areas' — fixed-rate grants are not available, but job-related assistance may be provided.

Every few years the areas with the most severe problems are identified. Fig. 119 shows the areas which the government feels should receive special assistance from 1982.

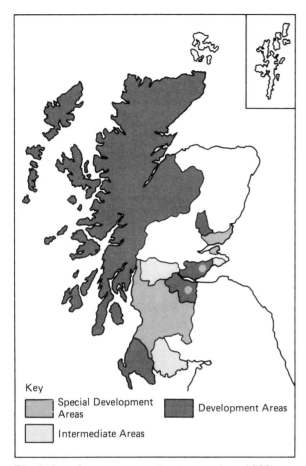

Key

□ Special Development Areas ■ Development Areas

□ Intermediate Areas

Fig. 119　　Government assisted areas since 1982

As well as providing money for factories and equipment the fund also makes aid available for the improvement of communications e.g. new roads necessary for industrial growth.

Success — then new problems
As a result of these measures, thousands of jobs have been created in a wide variety of **growth** industries like chemicals, food and drink, and electronics. Scotland has thus become less dependent on the old industries.

Unfortunately however energy costs have risen greatly since 1974, there has been a worldwide recession i.e. a cut back in trade and many factories have been forced to close down. Unemployment figures are therefore still rising fast.

Exercise

1 Examine Fig. 118.
　(a) Explain how (i) Government Regional Assistance, and (ii) Regional Development Agencies can help reverse the decline of industry in an area.
　(b) If the government measures are successful there will be an increase in the number of industries in the area. Draw a second diagram to indicate the effect this would have on the area as a whole.
　(c) Describe and explain the location of the Special Development Areas in Scotland today.

2. Regional Development Agencies have also been set up in order to encourage development in several parts of the U.K. — the two major ones in Scotland are:
(a) The Highlands and Islands Development Board (see Chapter 9);
(b) The Scottish Development Agency — which provides money and *advice* for industrialists, builders and managers, and aids new industrial estates (where industrialists may be allowed loans or temporary rent-free periods in an attempt to attract them to Scotland).

Aid from the E.E.C.
Since 1975, when the U.K. joined the European Economic Community, the Assisted Areas in Scotland have also received assistance from the European Regional Development Fund.

Electronics — a growth industry

One industry which has benefited greatly from government aid to Scotland is the electronics industry.

In 1943, an English firm, Ferranti, the biggest single employer in Scottish Electronics today, was set up in Scotland. They were followed by large American companies like Honeywell and I.B.M. Since then electronics has become one of Scotland's fastest growing industries with many smaller firms developing to supply the larger ones with components or make specialised products of their own. There are now over 200 companies in Scotland employing around 38 000 people (many of whom are scientists, engineers and technicians)

Fig. 120　A silicon chip

(b) Take each of the characteristics listed below and explain why each would help to encourage electronics companies to locate in this part of Scotland.

(i) It is much closer to Western Europe than the U.S.A. is.

(ii) Most of it has been either a Development Area or Special Development Area.

(iii) All five New Towns are here.

(iv) There are 65 establishments providing scientific, engineering and technical training schemes in Scotland, e.g. universities, technical colleges.

(v) The area has had a history of high unemployment.

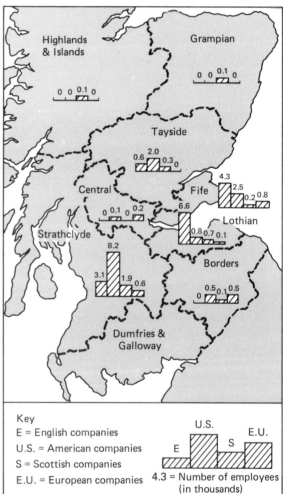

Fig. 121　Employment in electronics by regions (no's in '000s)

as well as encouraging the growth of several other firms supplying services or raw materials like sheet metals. As a result a wide range of products are now produced e.g. calculator chips, television sets, stereo-system components, radar systems, mini-computers and medical scanners, among other appliances used at home, in industry and in defence.

The most significant development in electronics has been the development of **micro-electronic** devices like the **silicon chip** i.e. a tiny piece of silicon on which inter-connected electronic circuits are built (Fig. 120). Smaller and smaller electronic devices are being built saving more and more money, increasing the efficiency of machines and wasting less storage space.

Exercise

1 Examine Fig. 121.
(a) In which of Scotland's three physical sections is the electronics industry concentrated?

(vi) There are no language barriers between Scotland, England and America.

(vii) The area has excellent rail and particularly road communications.

(viii) There is an adequate supply of workers skilled and experienced in electronic-related jobs.

2 Examine Fig. 121.

(a) How many people work in electronics in Strathclyde Region?

(b) In which region is employment in American Companies concentrated?

(c) In which two regions is employment in English Companies concentrated?

Percentage of total electronics employment

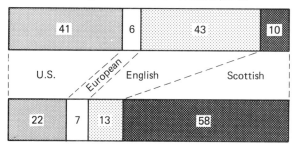

Fig. 122

3 Examine Fig. 122.

(a) What percentage of the people in Scotland working in electronics work for Scottish firms?

(b) What percentage of the electronics firms are **Scottish**?

(c) Suggest two possible reasons for this difference.

Destination market	% of products
Scotland	7
Rest of U.K.	55
Rest of Europe	26
U.S.	5
Rest of World	7
Total	100%

Fig. 123   Markets for electronic products made in Scotland

4 Examine Fig. 123 and write a short paragraph describing the information shown on it.

The electronics industry is not the only industry to have grown in Scotland recently. Those industries related to the extraction and production of North Sea oil have also developed. Unlike electronics however these industries have brought more employment to **other** parts of Scotland than they have to the Central Lowlands. (See Chapter 6).

6
North Sea oil and gas

One of the most important industrial developments in Scotland in recent years has been the discovery and extraction of oil and gas from the North Sea. Until 1975, most oil had to be imported, mainly from Middle Eastern countries like Kuwait, by huge ocean going tankers. The tankers landed the crude (raw) oil at the deep water terminal at Finnart (on Clydeport). The oil was then pumped 96 km by pipeline to Grangemouth to be refined. Nowadays however we need rely much less on Middle Eastern oil, although some is still imported since it is heavy oil and is much more suitable for certain purposes than the lighter North Sea oil.

In the past gas supplies were obtained from coal, then later from oil, but now natural gas is pumped directly from beneath the North Sea. Fortunately this gas gives out more heat but less pollution that the previous types.

Formation of oil and gas

Millions of years ago the remains of dead sea creatures sank to the bottom of the sea and became mixed with sediments (particles of rock broken off from the surrounding land areas). Over millions of years this mixture continually piled up resulting in great pressure and heat which gradually changed the dead remains into oil and gas and the rock sediments into solid rock. Although North Sea oil was formed in this way most North Sea gas was not. Scientists believe that earth movements squeezed this gas out of coal deposits lying far below the sea. Once formed the oil and gas squeezed upwards through pores in the rock until they reached 'traps' of impermeable rock. (See Fig. 124.)

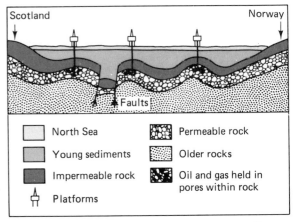

Fig. 124   Simplified section west-east across North Sea and sediments beneath

The early days

Although geologists realised that the sedimentary rocks beneath the North Sea might hold large quantities of oil and gas they also realised the enormity of the task of extraction, e.g. gales up to 200 km per hour; huge waves, often over 15 m high; extremely low temperatures; very deep waters; great distances from land.

Even when new technology designed to overcome such problems was developed, it was obvious that extraction of oil and gas from such an inhospitable area would be extremely costly. By the early 1960s however the surrounding countries decided that exploration should begin. Since all the countries bordering the North Sea wanted the benefits of oil and gas development, they had to get together and decide how the sea should be divided up. As a result the North Sea has been divided up into sectors, with each country controlling the exploration, drilling and

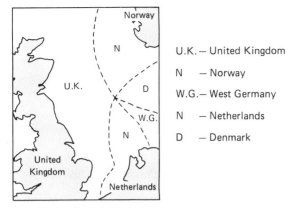

Fig. 125   North Sea — licensing sectors

U.K. — United Kingdom
N   — Norway
W.G. — West Germany
N   — Netherlands
D   — Denmark

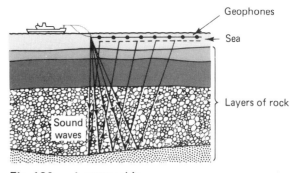

Fig. 126   A survey ship

production of their own sector (see Fig. 125). Each sector was also divided into smaller blocks and each country can offer licences to companies like B.P., Shell and Esso who wish to explore for oil and gas in these blocks. Although gas fields (we call an area of trapped oil or gas a **field**) were found fairly quickly the first worthwhile oilfield was not discovered until 1969.

Exploration

Since then several companies have bought licences to explore for oil and gas under the North Sea. Many have been successful (see Fig. 136 on p. 95) finding gas fields mainly in the southern half and oilfields mainly in the northern half.

Exploration is done in two stages, by surveying and drilling. A **survey ship** is sent out (see Fig. 126) towing a device which gives out sound waves which travel down through many layers of rock, these are reflected back upwards and are picked up on a string of devices called **geophones**. The results are fed into a computer which help the scientists decide whether an oil 'trap' or oilfield may be found below. The only way to be certain that

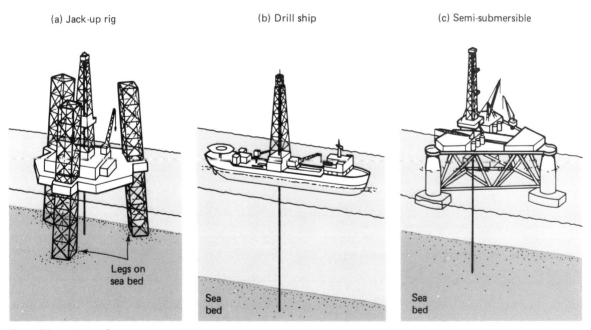

Fig. 127   North Sea rigs

89

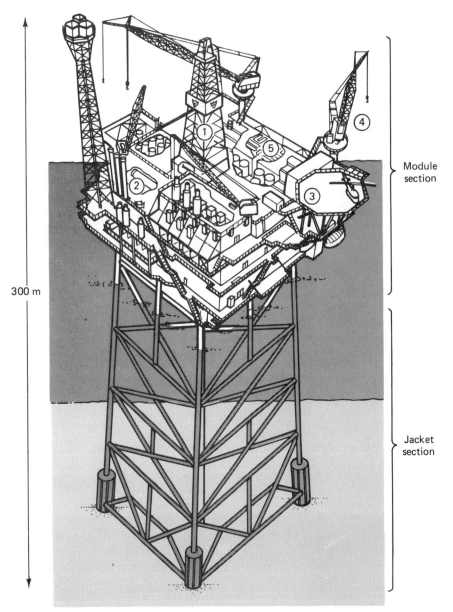

Module section

300 m

Jacket section

Fig. 128   Production platform

oil exists is to drill for it using a structure called an **oil rig**. To cope with the different conditions experienced in different parts of the North Sea three main types of **rig** have been developed (see Fig. 127).

1. Jack-up rig. This type is towed to the field where its legs are jacked to the sea bottom. Since it is not floating it is very **stable** but can only be used in **shallower** water.

2. Drill ship. These are very **mobile** and can be used in exceptionally deep water, since they need no anchor. They are kept in position by computer-controlled engines. They are less stable in stormy conditions than the jack-up rig and the semi-submersible.

3. Semi-submersible. As the name suggests, this is partly submerged beneath the sea and is tied to the sea-bed by anchors. Its hollow legs

are filled with water when drilling so it is very stable — when moving, water is pumped out. It is the most common type in the North Sea since it is stable and can be used in fairly deep water. The newer ones can move on their own.

Much time, effort and expense is spent on drilling for oil and gas but unfortunately only a few drills actually find them in the 'caps' discovered by the survey vessels. Even if oil or gas is found, various laboratory tests are undertaken to establish whether fields will be 'commercial' i.e. whether a profit can be made.

Extraction of oil and gas

The extraction phase is carried out by huge **production platforms** made of steel or concrete such as that shown in Fig. 128. Unlike rigs these huge platforms are more or less permanently fixed to the sea-bed and so must be extremely large and strong (many are over 300 m from top to sea-bed). Usually several platforms are anchored over a field and since each platform can bore over 30 drill holes vast quantities of oil can be brought up from beneath the sea-bed at one time. A platform requires many skilled people working together doing different jobs to help the oil run smoothly; e.g. supervisors, helicopter pilots, drillers, divers (to check equipment beneath the sea), crane operators, welders and cooks.

All work long hours, many in dangerous and demanding conditions, but all are highly paid for this work.

As Fig. 128 shows the **production platform** consists of **two sections** i.e. the **module section (top)** and the **jacket section (bottom)**.

Module section
This usually contains several sophisticated compartments called modules and include:
1. Drilling equipment
2. Equipment for pumping, for regulating oil flow and separating oil, gas and water.
3. Helicopter pad
4. Supply cranes and fittings
5. Living quarters (with bedrooms, dining room, games room, bar etc.) often accommodating 200 people.

Jacket section
This section supports the module and drilling equipment above the hostile sea below. The **modules** and **jacket** of a platform are usually constructed on different sites on the mainland (see Fig. 136 on p. 95). The jacket is built on a raft and floated out to the field. Once there, the raft is gradually allowed to fill up with water which tilts the jacket and glides it upright onto the sea-bed (see Fig. 129). The jacket is then secured to the sea-bed using steel piles and the raft is removed. The modules are transported out by ship then

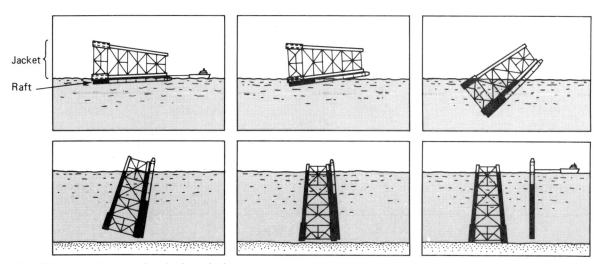

Fig. 129   Positioning of a platform jacket

lifted by crane onto the top of the jacket then welded securely to it (Fig. 130).

Transportation

After extraction the oil and gas must be transported to the mainland from the production platforms. Unfortunately the hostility of the sea off Scotland makes it very difficult for large tankers to dock near the platforms, so many companies find it more economical to pump the oil and gas through submarine (underwater) pipelines to the mainland.

It would cost far too much to build a pipeline from each platform to the shore so the oil is usually pumped to one main platform from all the others in the oilfield, then pumped through one pipeline to the shore (Fig. 131).

Fig. 130   Module being placed on jacket in North Sea

Fig. 131

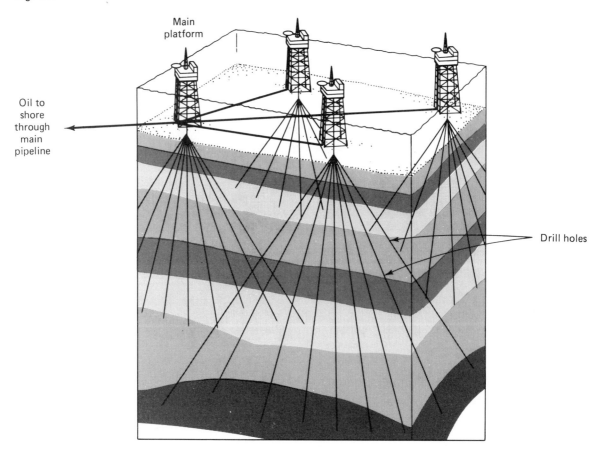

These pipelines must be able to withstand the great pressure exerted by the water above, and rocks and currents which may knock against them on the sea-bed. As a result they are made of steel, coated with tar (to reduce corrosion or wearing away) then with concrete for added strength and weight. After construction and coating, the lengths of pipeline are taken out on a ship, welded together and steadily lowered into the sea, in a continuous string.

The pipe-laying ship resembles a spider spinning a length of its web (Fig. 132). After laying, the pipeline is 'trenched' into the sea-bed using special jetting machinery and then inspected by divers.

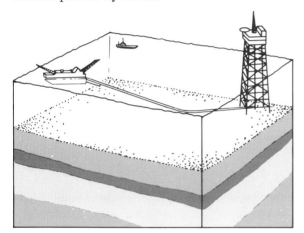

Fig. 132

Exercise

1 Describe in at least 50 words how oil and gas were formed beneath the North Sea. Your answer should include the following words: pressure; sea creatures; sediments; impermeable rock.

2 (a) Where did Scotland obtain (i) oil and (ii) gas before the North Sea deposits were discovered?
(b) Describe two advantages the New Natural Gas has over the older types.

3 (a) Which countries other than the United Kingdom can offer licences to drill for oil and gas in the North Sea?
(b) Suggest why the British sector is larger than all the others.

4 'The North Sea is one of the most hostile environments oil men have ever had to face.' List four problems that had to be overcome before oil could be drilled in the North Sea.

5 (a) Name the three types of rig in Fig. 133 which have been used to drill for oil in the North Sea.
(b) Which of the three is now most commonly used in the North Sea?
(c) Give two advantages this type of rig has over the others for North Sea drilling.

Fig. 133

6 Examine Fig. 128.

(a) Draw a simple sketch of this platform (include the scale).

(b) Find out the height of your school then draw your school on the same scale beside the diagram.

(c) How do the two structures compare in size?

7 Describe and explain what is happening in Figs. 134 and 135.

Fig. 134

Fig. 135

8 (a) Explain why pipelines rather than tankers are used by most companies to transport oil from the northern parts of the North Sea to the mainland.

(b) Explain why these pipelines are so expensive to build and lay.

9 (a) Give the meaning of the terms module and jacket.

(b) List some of the jobs that are carried out on an oil platform.

Onshore developments

All this activity in the North Sea has had a marked effect on Scotland's landscape. Fig. 136 illustrates some of the major onshore developments which have occurred as a result. They include: oil and gas terminals e.g. Sullom Voe, Flotta, Cruden Bay; construction yards e.g. Nigg Bay, Loch Kishorn; service bases e.g. Aberdeen, Peterhead.

Oil/gas terminals

Fig. 136 shows that each pipeline eventually ends up at an onshore **terminal**. Here the water, gas and oil coming through the pipeline is separated. The oil and gas are then stored in tanks ready for transport by tanker, road, rail or another pipeline to a refinery. In the St. Fergus gas terminal impurities are removed then the gas is fed into the National Grid — a network of pipelines which supplies gas to consumers all over the country — or is transported by pipeline directly to a gas processing plant at Mossmorran.

Construction yards

In order to exploit the vast reserves of oil and gas beneath the North Sea, millions of pounds worth of rigs, platforms, ships and pipelines have had to be constructed — many of a completely new design, to cope with the special problems of extracting oil from beneath such a rough deep sea. Many of Scotland's sheltered deep water estuaries and harbours provide ideal conditions for their construction (see Fig. 136).

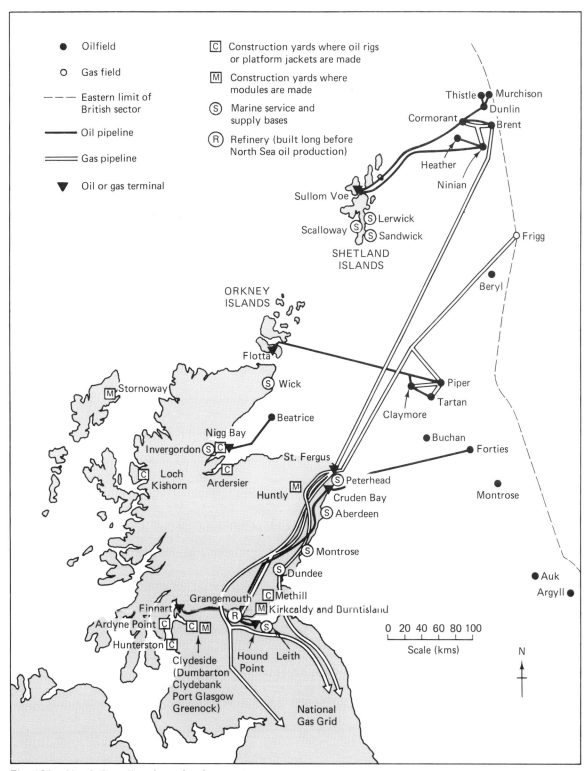

Fig. 136   North Sea oil and gas developments

Service and supply bases e.g. Aberdeen and Peterhead

The rigs and platforms lying out in the North Sea cannot exist on their own. There must be bases on the mainland from where men, machinery, pipes, food, clothing, medicine and other materials needed for the production of North Sea oil and gas, can be transported either by ship or helicopter. In addition the rigs may have to be brought to the mainland for repair and servicing. The centre which took most advantage of such needs was Aberdeen. (See Fig. 137.)

Although Aberdeen did not provide the **ideal** location for a supply base it became 'Europe's Oil Capital' for several reasons. Its nearness to the oilfields allowed efficient control of offshore operations. It had a

Fig. 137   Aberdeen harbour showing supply vessels

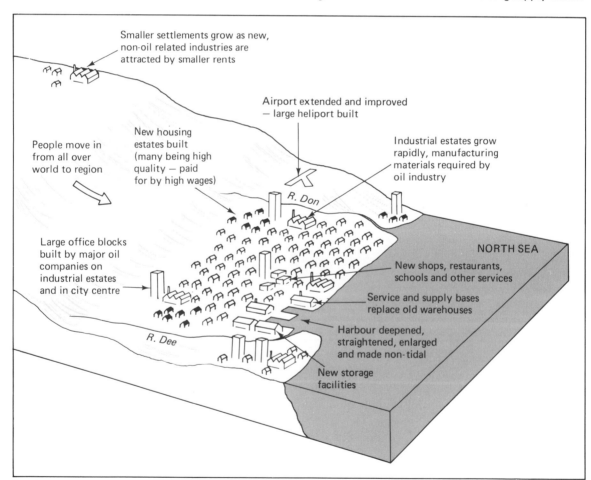

Smaller settlements grow as new, non-oil related industries are attracted by smaller rents

Airport extended and improved — large heliport built

People move in from all over world to region

New housing estates built (many being high quality — paid for by high wages)

Industrial estates grow rapidly, manufacturing materials required by oil industry

Large office blocks built by major oil companies on industrial estates and in city centre

R. Don

NORTH SEA

New shops, restaurants, schools and other services

Service and supply bases replace old warehouses

Harbour deepened, straightened, enlarged and made non-tidal

R. Dee

New storage facilities

Fig. 138   Aberdeen — the effects of North Sea oil

harbour which could be expanded and strengthened. It had **shipbuilding** and repair facilities, as well as storage space in the dock area. Most important however it had an **airport** capable of taking jet aircraft and capable of expansion. (It now has a large **heliport** so people can be transported quickly to and from oil platforms.) As a result Aberdeen has become the focus for management, services, supplies and communications for the offshore industry. The great changes which have taken place to the city's landscape in the last fifteen years are shown in Fig. 138.

Eventually the oil will reach a **refinery**, whether at home or abroad. On reaching the refinery the raw or **crude oil** is still in fact a mixture of several materials, many of which are useful. When this **crude oil** enters the refinery it is heated to very high temperatures and since each of the constituents or **fractions** has a different boiling point, they can be separated out, as shown in Fig. 139.

After leaving the **fractionating tower** each **fraction** can be processed to form an enormous variety of products. A few of these products are shown in Fig. 139 and illustrate the importance of oil to society. The only oil refinery in Scotland today is the British Petroleum (B.P.) refinery at Grangemouth, around which has grown a huge petrochemicals complex (see Fig. 140).

Although this refinery now receives most of its oil from the **Forties Field**, it existed long before any North Sea oil was discovered. There were several reasons for its construction on this site in 1924:
1. There was a growing **market** for petroleum products in Scotland, North-East England and Scandinavia (to the east).
2. The **site** provided an area of cheap flat land.
3. Grangemouth was already an important **port** at the eastern end of the Forth/Clyde Canal controlling much of the movement of raw materials and manufactures in and out of Central Scotland.
4. **Labour** skilled in oil technology was available since oil had been obtained from **shale** in the nearby Lothian area for many years.

One eventual **disadvantage** of this location however was that Grangemouth harbour was not deep enough to take the huge oil tankers which brought much of the crude oil from the Middle East. As a result these tankers have to transport the Middle-Eastern oil to the deep water terminal at **Finnart** on **Clydeport**, from where it is carried by pipelines to Grangemouth.

The products from the refinery are transported by road, rail, sea (through the port of Grangemouth) and pipeline to a number of depots, terminals, factories and garages throughout Scotland.

The petrochemical industry now employs around 28 000 people and is becoming increasingly important throughout Scotland. Due to the location of the refinery however there is a concentration of such industries within the Grangemouth area itself, the companies being attracted by the availability of the refined fractions which they use as raw materials (see Fig. 141).

Note: not all of the oil from the Forties Field goes into the refinery. After entering the gas separation plant most is piped to the storage tank farm at Dalmeny then exported via the Hound Point terminal to other refineries in the U.K. and overseas (see inset in Fig. 141).

Pollution control
The word pollution means 'spoiling of the landscape' and the oil and gas industry is often associated with this word, perhaps justifiably so. Oil developments may cause several types of pollution:
1. The ugly buildings which make up a refinery or terminal or even pipelines often spoil the look of the landscape;
2. As a result of processing, gases are released into the atmosphere, many containing harmful elements and producing unpleasant smells;
3. The noise created during construction and processing may disturb local people;
4. Local wildlife may be affected, for example the oil developments may disturb birds during the breeding season;
5. Local waters may be polluted, either by waste products being released from refineries and terminals, or by tankers having accidents

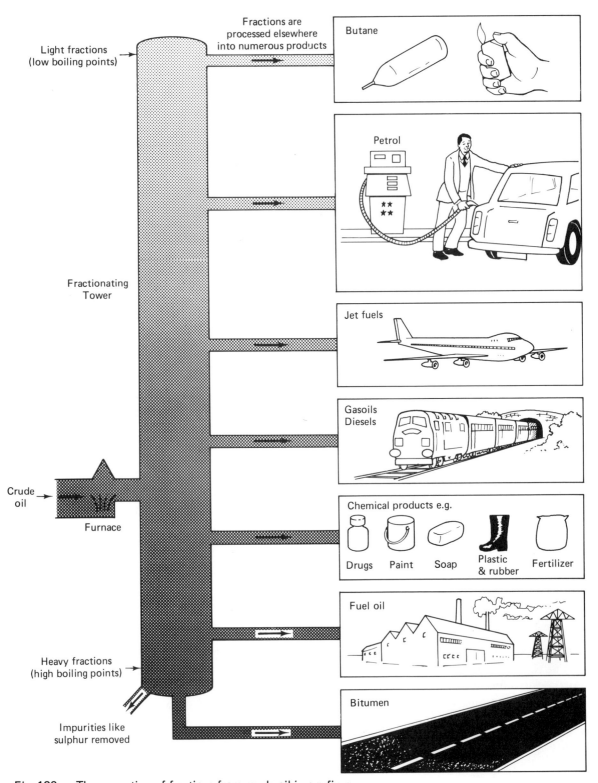

Fig. 139   The separation of fractions from crude oil in a refinery

and spilling oil into the sea. This can ruin beaches and kill fish, birds and other animals e.g. sheep feeding on seaweed. The livelihood of local fishermen may be threatened.

Nowadays however the oil and gas companies have special planning departments who carry out certain measures to ensure that the harm caused by oil and gas developments is kept to a minimum:

1. Artificial hills are built or trees grown to hide the buildings and keep in any noise — many buildings are faced with local stone or painted green to blend in with the local scenery. Many of the pipelines and some storage facilities are buried beneath the ground which is then reseeded with grass.

2. To reduce the effects of gas high chimneys are built so that it is dispersed high into the atmosphere and blown away. Many have filters on them which trap the most harmful elements.

3. Terminals and refineries are usually built away from large built-up areas so that as few people as possible are disturbed.

4. Great care is taken to avoid constructing buildings where they would disturb breeding grounds or migration routes of birds or other animals.

5. Oil companies now have extremely specialised equipment for dealing with emergencies like oil spillage, e.g. dispersants have been developed to break up the oil slicks and much research has gone into making sure that few emergencies take place in the future, e.g. new safer routes are taken by tankers when entering or leaving the terminals. Most waste products from refineries are now chemically treated to render them harmless before they are released into the sea.

All companies must now provide full details of the methods they intend to use to reduce

Fig. 140   Grangemouth refinery and gas separation plant

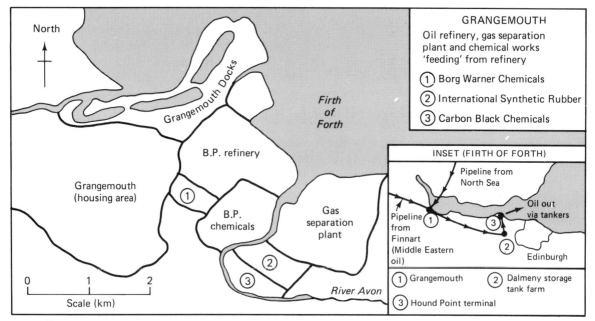

Fig. 141

landscape damage before any construction begins. Discussions are held with local authorities and other interested people e.g. local fishermen, who, if they object, can have a public enquiry where they are given a chance to state their argument to the Secretary of State.

Conclusion

The development of North Sea oil and gas has had a tremendous effect on Scotland in the last fifteen years, and although such development has lead to problems of pollution, alteration to traditional ways of life and conflicts over land-use, it has brought tremendous advantages which most people would agree outweigh the disadvantages. Namely:

1. The United Kingdom is less dependent on oil from other countries and so is much less affected by changes in the price and availability of their oil;

2. Approximately 80 000 people are now working in North Sea oil and gas related jobs;

3. As a result many areas which were at one time losing people and declining are now attracting them and prospering;

4. The developments have brought foreign money into the country, and so benefits the Balance of Payments;

5. Although North Sea oil and gas reserves are unlikely to last far beyond the early years of next century they now provide a dependable source of energy which should help keep the country going until other energy sources e.g. nuclear energy, are sufficiently developed to take over.

Exercise

Examine Fig. 136 and answer the questions below:

1 (a) Fig. 142 shows the oil terminal on Shetland, the largest oil terminal in Europe. Name this terminal.

(b) From which oilfields is this terminal supplied with oil?

(c) How is the oil transported from these fields to the terminal?

(d) Suggest the purpose of features labelled A and B on Fig. 142.

(e) To which type of oil-related development does the oil go after leaving the terminal?

(f) How is it transported there?

(g) Suggest three reasons why this was a suitable site and situation for an oil terminal. Your answer should refer to two points about its site (from the

Fig. 142

photograph) and one point about its situation
(from the map).
(h) What other oil-related developments have been
built on Shetland?
(i) Many Shetlanders objected strongly when plans
for these developments were announced. Write a
paragraph of at least 100 words to explain why.
(Clue — Shetland, until 1970, was a quiet group of
islands where most people were employed in
agriculture, fishing and small-scale textile
manufacture.)
(j) The oil developments did however bring certain
advantages to the people of the islands. Suggest
what some of these advantages might be.

2 Fig. 143(a) shows an area of countryside near
Aberdeen during the laying of the oil pipeline from
the Forties Field to Grangemouth refinery. Fig.
143(b) shows the same area after the pipeline had
been laid. Describe the measures which have been
taken to ensure the pipeline causes minimum damage
to the environment.

Fig. 143(a)

Fig. 143(b)

3 (a) In Grangemouth refinery the crude oil is 'fractionated'. Explain what this means and how this is achieved.

(b) List at least six products which can be made from the fractions produced in an oil refinery.

(c) Explain in your own words why this site was chosen for an oil refinery.

(d) Grangemouth refinery has received oil from other sources for many years. Name one other source of oil and the terminal through which it is imported.

(e) Why was the construction of this terminal necessary when the port of Grangemouth is much nearer the refinery?

(f) The docks at Grangemouth are still very important for the refinery however. Explain why.

4 Examine Fig. 140 and with the help of Fig. 141 answer the following questions:

(a) In which direction was the camera facing when the photograph was taken? (choose from north-west, north-east, south-west, south-east);

(b) In what direction was the wind blowing?

(c) Explain your answer to (b).

(d) Why would this fact be disturbing to many people living in Grangemouth?

(e) Explain the function of the feature labelled X.

(f) Name power stations Y and Z on the far side of the Firth of Forth (Fig. 97 may help you to answer this).

(g) What fuel do these stations use?

(h) New docks (W) had to be built projecting out into the Firth of Forth to allow Grangemouth to develop as an important port. Explain why, using evidence from the photograph.

5 Despite being so far away from the North Sea, there are several sites where rigs and platforms are constructed on the west coast of Scotland. Name two such sites and suggest why they are located on the west coast rather than on the east coast.

6 There is no pipeline leading from the Montrose field to the mainland.

(a) How then is the oil transported from this field?

(b) Why is this method of transporting the oil from the North Sea platforms less popular than transport by pipeline?

7 (a) Explain in your own words why Aberdeen developed as a modern supply and service base for North Sea platforms.

(b) Using Fig. 138, describe in at least 150 words how the city's landscape has been altered as a result of North Sea oil.

(c) Suggest some benefits these changes will have brought to the people of Aberdeen.

(d) Although the majority of Aberdonians welcomed the arrival of the North Sea oil developments to their city certain problems have been caused. Using the following clues make a list of possible problems.

1 Although fishing was already declining before the arrival of oil there were still many fishing vessels using the harbour and local waters.

2 There has been a dramatic increase in the price of houses in Aberdeen.

3 North Sea oil will not last forever.

4 The incomers may be used to a completely different lifestyle.

Fig. 144

Region	No. employed in oil related developments (in 000's)
Grampian	34
Highland and W. Isles	7
Orkney and Shetland	2
Tayside	2
Lothian, Fife, Central and Strathclyde	5
Total	50

8 (a) Examine Fig. 144 then copy and complete the bar diagram, Fig. 145.

(b) Explain the distribution of employment shown on the bar diagram.

(c) Many people working in oil and gas related jobs never have to leave the mainland. Suggest four types of job these people may have.

(d) Try to explain what is meant by the U.K.'s Balance of Payments.

(e) Construct a table headed 'North Sea Oil Development' with two columns labelled advantages and disadvantages to Scotland, and list as many items in each column as you can.

Distribution of Employment in Scotland wholly associated with N. Sea Oil — by percentage

Fig. 145

= Grampian

= Highlands and W. Isles

= Orkney and Shetland

= Tayside

= Lothian, Fife, Central and Strathclyde

7
Transport and electricity supplies

Transport facilities act as a country's 'bloodstream' carrying materials from one area to another. If this bloodstream does not function properly, a large part or even the whole of the country suffers. The four main methods of transporting people or goods in Scotland today are rail, road, air, and sea.

Railways and roads

When todays 'old' industrial landscapes were developing in the 19th century, there were no motor cars or aircraft to carry people or goods quickly from one part of the country to another, and despite some competition from canals, the railways were by far the most efficient means of transport. During this century however, the railways have lost great amounts of money due largely to the rise in competition from road transport. Whereas road vehicles can transport goods or people direct from door to door, trains are less flexible. Most factories and homes have roads leading to them, but very few have a railway. As a result, most people and goods travelling by train eventually transfer to some form of road transport e.g. bus, car, or lorry. The railways are most efficient however when bulky materials have to be transported long distances overland. In this case the transfer of goods to a form of road transport near the goods' destination point is not such a disadvantage. Furthermore, many people prefer to travel by train than to drive on busy roads. As a result railways still have an important part to play in society today.

What has been done to increase the efficiency of railways?
The government, recognising the importance of a railway network, has taken several steps to ensure its efficiency and so prevent decline.
1. In 1948 Britain's railways were **nationalised** so that there would be less wasteful competition between different railway companies.
2. Many unprofitable lines and stations have been closed down.
3. Steam trains have been replaced by diesel and electric trains which are cleaner, faster, more comfortable and cheaper to run.
4. Freightliners have been developed i.e. trains designed to carry containers (large standardised 'metal boxes' used in ports like Grangemouth (Fig. 147)). These containers can be transported to ships or lorries by standardised cranes, and so allow very quick changeovers to take place without disturbing their contents.

Problems of road transport

The rapid development of motorized road transport this century has caused the old road systems in Scotland to become greatly congested since they were not built to take the huge amounts of traffic which travel along them today.

The problem of traffic congestion is at its worst in the towns and cities of Scotland, since this is where most people live, work and travel. Pages 53 and 54 describe the problems of congestion and the measures which can be taken to reduce such problems.

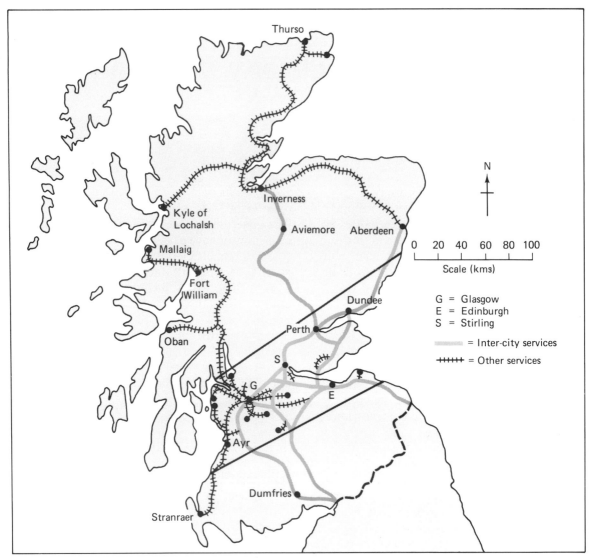

Fig. 146   British Rail principal passenger network in Scotland

Fig. 147   A freightliner railhead

Exercise

1 (a) Examine Figs. 146 and 148 and copy and
      complete the following sentences choosing your
      answers from: Highlands; Southern Uplands;
      Central Lowlands.

   The area of Scotland best served by roads and
   railways is the _____ _____ . 'A' class roads and
   the main railway lines are more thinly spread over
   the _____ and _____ _____ . Furthermore, the
   only area with motorways is the _____ _____ .
   1 mark

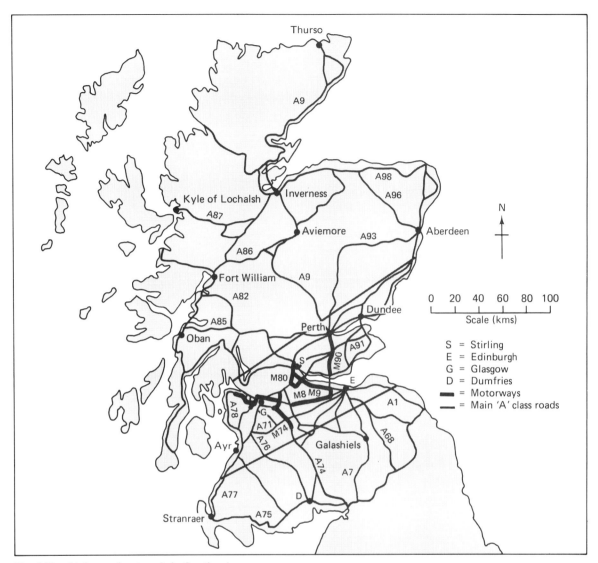

Fig. 148   Main road network in Scotland

(b) Write a short paragraph of 50 words explaining your answer to (a) using the following clues: height and slope of land; distribution of population and industry; greater need for roads and railways in some areas. *3 marks*

2 (a) In the Highlands and Southern Uplands the roads and railways tend to follow the same routes, e.g. many run along the coastal plains. Which other type of natural routeway do the roads and railways follow in these areas? (See Fig. 1.) *1 mark*
(b) Even coastal roads and railways in the Central Lowlands are diverted by natural obstacles. Suggest what these 'obstacles' are. (Clues — there are three major ones in Central Scotland. Examine the Edinburgh-Aberdeen railway line.) *½ mark*
(c) Give two ways in which these 'obstacles' have been conquered to some extent. *1 mark*
(d) Why have fewer similar measures been taken to solve the same problem in the Highlands? *1 mark*

3 Most of the railways shown as thin lines on Fig. 146 are making a loss and yet they have not been closed down. Suggest a reason for this. *1 mark*

4 Explain what is meant by the following terms

naming the nearest example of each to your school:
(a) motorway; (b) dual carriageway; (c) trunk road.
3 marks

5 (a) Which part of your town becomes most
congested with traffic? *½ mark*
(b) At which time(s) is this congestion at its
worst? *½ mark*
(c) Describe the measures which have been taken
to reduce this congestion (if any). *1 mark*

	Roads	Railways
1		
2		
3		
4		
5		

Fig. 149   Road and rail transport — a comparison

6 Copy and complete Fig. 149 using the phrases A–J:

A faster over short distances
B faster over long distances
C developed mainly in the 19th century
D developed mainly in the 20th century
E main problem is congestion
F main problem is inflexibility
G leads right to destination
H seldom leads right to destination
I more efficient with small quantities of goods or
people
J more efficient with large quantities of goods or
people *5 marks*

7 Roads and railways not only compete but 'integrate'
i.e. work together (to the advantage of both of them)
in order to make communications more efficient.
Give one example of such an arrangement. *1 mark*

8 Suggest which method of transport, road or rail
would be most suitable for:
(a) A businessman travelling from the CBD of
Glasgow to the CBD of London.
(b) A family holiday in the Highlands.
(c) Delivery of perishable foods from a warehouse
to a shop.
(d) A commuter from Dunfermline to Edinburgh.
(e) Supplies of coal from Monktonhall mine to
Cockenzie Power Station. *2½ marks*

9 While road transport is becoming increasingly
important in this country today, rail transport has
experienced a decline. Try to find any evidence for
these trends in your local area and describe this
evidence. *3 marks*

Total 25 marks

Network analysis

You may have noticed, while waiting in a bus,
train or underground station that there are
maps on the walls showing the major routes
and stations through which you can travel.
These are not proper maps. Can you suggest
how they differ from real maps?

Usually these diagrams show the railways as
straight lines and the stations as dots with

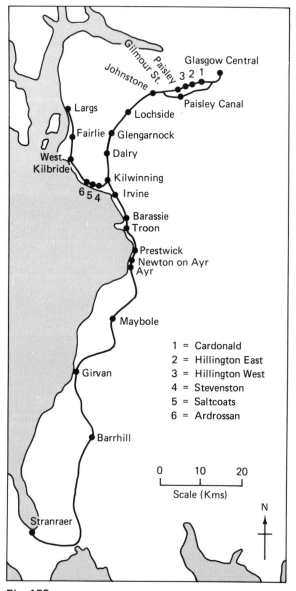

Fig. 150

106

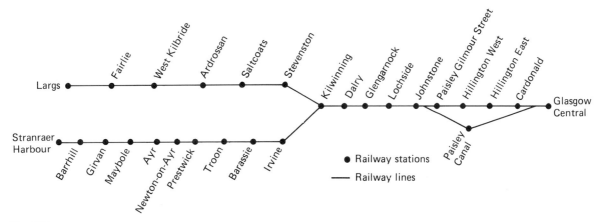

Fig. 151

their names beside them. These diagrams **do not show the direction or distance between stations accurately**. Examine Figs. 150 and 151. They show the railway lines linking Glasgow with the Ayrshire Coast, but while Fig. 150 is a proper map i.e. with scale and direction, Fig. 151 is obviously less accurate but it does have an advantage for the ordinary passenger. Can you suggest what this is?

Diagrams similar to Fig. 151 are called **topological diagrams** and as well as being useful to railway passengers they can be used to study the patterns made by transport networks. It is important to understand the following two terms when using such diagrams:

1. **Nodes** (or **vertices**) – these are shown by **dots** on the diagram and represent (a) stations or towns (b) points where the railways or roads meet (junctions) (c) points where the railways or roads end or (d) points where the roads or railways leave the map.

2. **Edges** – these are shown by **lines** (usually straight) and represent the railways or roads. **Note**: when drawing a topological diagram all edges must lead to and from a node and scale and direction are unimportant. All the nodes and edges however must be shown in the same **order** as on a real map.

On O.S. maps it may happen that within a town's boundary there are several road junctions. If this happens count them all under **one** node i.e. a town unless asked

otherwise e.g. on O.S. Map 3 there are several junctions within Kelso. These are all counted as **one node**. It is usually only the larger towns/villages that are recorded as nodes.

Exercise

1 Copy Fig. 151.
   (a) Add the two **nodes** which are missed out to convert it into a proper topological diagram.
   (b) State how many **nodes** and **edges** you can see.

2 Draw topological diagrams of the two networks shown in Fig. 152 (use straight lines for edges).

3 (a) Examine O.S. Map 3 and draw a topological diagram of the railway network shown on it (use straight lines for edges).
   (b) How many **nodes** and **edges** do you have on your diagram?

4 Examine O.S. Map 3 again and Fig. 153.
   (a) Which of the three diagrams in Fig. 153 is a suitable topological diagram of the 'A' class road network shown on the map? (There could be one, two or three suitable diagrams.)
   (b) Explain why there can be more than one suitable diagram.
   (c) If any of the three diagrams is **unsuitable** explain **why**. Give at least three reasons for your answer.
   (d) Why is it not possible to measure the distance between Melrose and Kelso using a topological diagram?

107

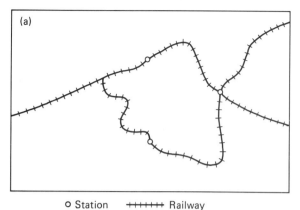

o Station　+++++++ Railway	● Town　————— 'A' class road

Fig. 152

The integration (or connectivity) of a network

To find out how well connected or integrated places are in a network a topological diagram is drawn and then a simple calculation called the **Beta Index** is used.

To calculate this **Beta Index** the following formula is used:

$$\text{BETA INDEX} = \frac{\text{EDGES}}{\text{NODES}} \text{ OR } \beta = \frac{E}{N}$$

If the answer to this simple calculation is:
(a) More than 1 this means that the network is well integrated i.e. the places are **well** connected and there is a good choice of routes between places.
(b) Equal to 1 this means that although the

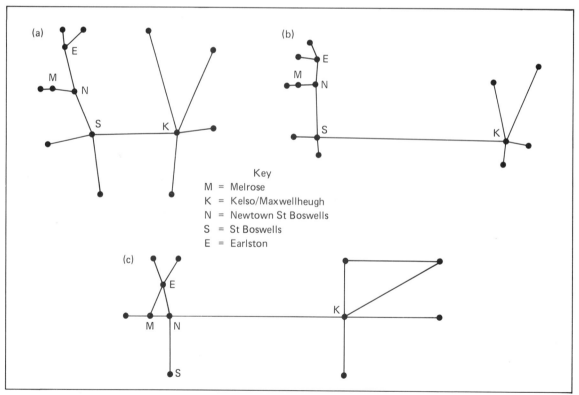

Key
M = Melrose
K = Kelso/Maxwellheugh
N = Newtown St Boswells
S = St Boswells
E = Earlston

Fig. 153

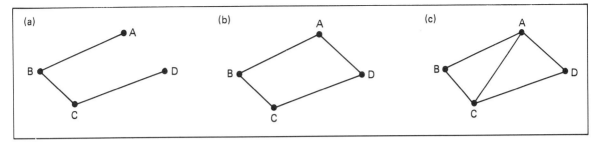

Fig. 154

places are not particularly well connected there is at least a choice of routes between most places in the network.

(c) Less than 1 this means that the network is poorly integrated i.e. the places are **poorly** connected and there is no choice of routes between places.

The higher the Beta Index the better the connections between places.

Examine the networks in Fig. 154, the nodes A, B, C, D are towns and the edges are roads.

The network in Fig. 154(a) has three edges and four nodes. Substitute these numbers into the Beta Index.

$$\text{BETA INDEX} = \frac{E}{N} = \frac{3}{4} = 0.75$$

i.e. it is less than 1 - the towns are poorly connected —there is no choice of route between each town.

In Fig. 154(b) the extra road built from A-D improves the situation.

$$\text{BETA INDEX} = \frac{E}{N} = \frac{4}{4} = 1$$

Now the towns are better connected and there is now a choice of routes between each town.

Another extra road in Fig. 154(c) running from A-C improves the network even more.

$$\text{BETA INDEX} = \frac{E}{N} = \frac{5}{4} = 1.25$$

Now the towns are even better connected — there is a greater choice of routes between the towns.

Exercise

1 (a) How many possible routes are there between town A and town C in each of the three diagrams in Fig. 154?
   (b) Is it possible to say which of the routes from A to C would be used most in diagram (b)?
   (c) Explain your answer.

● Stations　 Railways

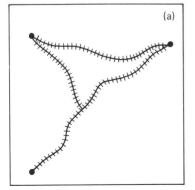
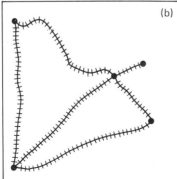
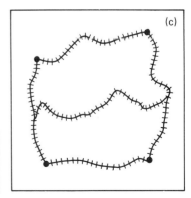

Fig. 155

109

2 (a) The network (Fig. 154(c)) could be improved even more by building another road to connect two of the towns. Draw a fourth diagram with this extra road included.
(b) Calculate the Beta Index of this new network (be careful with the number of nodes) to see if the integration of the network has improved.

3 Use the Beta Index to find out whether one of the railway networks in Fig. 155 is more integrated than the others. (**Remember to produce a topological diagram of each**).

4 Examine O.S. Map 3 and Fig. 153(a).
(a) Calculate the Beta Index of this network.
(b) Is this a well integrated network?
(c) Suggest how the integration of this network could be improved.
(d) Suggest two reasons why this has not happened.

The efficiency of routes within a network

Ideal roads or railways would be built in a **straight line** (the shortest distance between two points) so that travel from one place to another would be as quick as possible. In reality however roads and railways are seldom straight — they have to avoid steep hills, large estuaries, seas and other obstacles and so the **shortest** route between two places is seldom 100% efficient.

In order to calculate the directness or efficiency of a route the **Detour Index** is used.

$$\text{DETOUR INDEX} = \frac{\text{ACTUAL LENGTH OF ROUTE}}{\text{STRAIGHT LINE (DIRECT) DISTANCE}} \times \frac{100}{1}$$

For example the shortest route between Edinburgh and Glenrothes is 51 km while the direct distance is 26 km.

So the
$$\text{DETOUR INDEX} = \frac{51}{26} \times \frac{100}{1} = 196 \text{ (to the nearest whole number)}$$

Note: the Detour Index is always equal to or more than 100, since the actual route distance cannot be shorter than the direct distance

(Fig. 156). The higher the **Detour Index** the less direct or efficient the route i.e. the greater the detour the route makes.

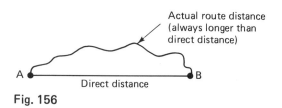

Actual route distance (always longer than direct distance)

A   Direct distance   B

Fig. 156

Exercise

1 (a) The shortest road route between Edinburgh and Falkirk is 40 km and the straight line distance is 37 km. Calculate the Detour Index of this route.
(b) How does this road compare with that from Edinburgh to Glenrothes?

2 Examine Fig. 157 and the text below, then answer questions (a)–(d).

Before the construction of the Kincardine Bridge in 1936 people travelling by road from Edinburgh to Kirkcaldy had to drive several kilometres west and up to Stirling cross the river and then drive back eastwards to Kirkcaldy. The only alternative was to cross the Forth by car ferry from Queensferry to North Queensferry. Despite the short distance across, a great deal of time was spent waiting, loading and unloading from the ferry especially in summer.

The construction of the Kincardine Bridge reduced this detour greatly but as the road traffic increased in the 1950s congestion on the Kincardine Bridge and vehicle ferry became too great so a new bridge had to be built. This time the site was between North Queensferry and Queensferry — and the Forth Road Bridge was built in 1964. The motorist from Edinburgh can now reach Kirkcaldy (and the rest of the towns in the North East) more quickly.

(a) Fig. 157 shows the shortest road distances between selected towns/villages around the Firth of Forth. Use the figures to calculate the Detour Index for the route between Edinburgh and

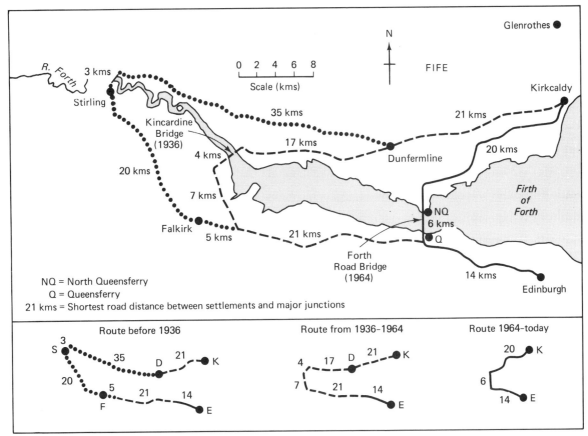

Fig. 157   Routes from Edinburgh to Kirkcaldy

Kirkcaldy:
  (i) Before 1936;
  (ii) Between 1936 and 1964;
  (iii) After 1964.

(Remember to use the scale of the map to find the direct distance.)

(b) Which of the three routes between Kirkcaldy and Edinburgh is therefore the most direct: via Stirling, via the Kincardine Bridge or via the Forth Road Bridge?

(c) Suggest what effect the building of the Forth Road Bridge would have on the amount of traffic using the Kincardine Bridge and the roads leading to it.

(d) Explain the following statements
  (i) 'The number of commuters living in Fife and working in Edinburgh has increased markedly since the opening of the Forth Road Bridge in 1964.'
  (ii) 'The Forth Road Bridge has been vitally

important to the development of industry in Glenrothes New Town.'

3 Examine O.S. Map 6 and answer the questions below.

(a) The Forth Road Bridge was not the first bridge to be built between Queensferry and North Queensferry. A bridge had already been built in 1890. Using your map state how this bridge differs from the Forth Road Bridge.

(b) Suggest why this bridge was built before a road bridge.

(c) Explain why this site was chosen for the bridges rather than a site further east or west.

(d) What steps have been taken to relieve traffic congestion in square 1277 — the south end of the Forth Road Bridge.

(e) Examine the aerial photograph of the Forth Bridges (Fig. 158). In which direction was the camera facing?

111

Fig. 158   The Forth Bridges

(f) Name —
  (i) Bridges A and B
  (ii) Settlements C and D
  (iii) Road E
  (iv) Firth F

(g) Three **motorways** are shown on this map extract.
  (i) Name these motorways;
  (ii) Write down three ways in which a motorway differs from an ordinary road;
  (iii) What then is the major advantage of such motorways to the car driver?
  (iv) The M8 leaves the map in square 0270. To which city in the West of Scotland does it eventually lead?
  (v) Why are great efforts made to build motorways on level ground?
  (vi) Write down three ways in which the M8 is kept relatively level — give grid references for each answer.

Sea ports

A **port** can be described simply as a point where goods (or people) are transferred between a sea-going vessel and land. Fig. 159 shows the main ports in Scotland.

Exercise

1 The total trade of a port is measured by adding the value of its imports and its exports. Explain what is meant by **imports** and **exports**.

2 Some of the ports shown in Fig. 159 were much less significant in the early 1970s than they are today. Even now virtually all their trade consists of handling one particular material.
  (a) Suggest what this material might be;
  (b) List the names of at least two ports whose

112

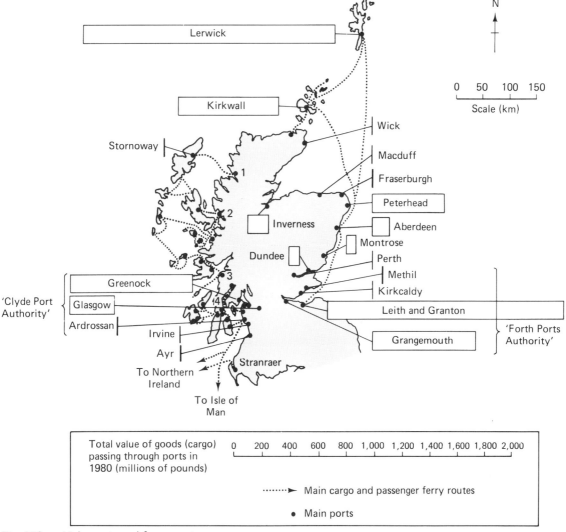

Fig. 159   Main ports and ferry routes

importance you think will have been greatly affected by the handling of this material.
(c) For most other cargoes the ports of the Central Lowlands are more important. Name the four main ports in the Central Lowlands.

3 On Fig. 159 the small ports numbered 1–4 on the west coast are not very important in terms of the amount of cargo they handle. They do however have important functions.
(a) Name the ports from your atlas;
(b) Suggest what their other important function may be using evidence from the map;
(c) Most of these ports are much busier during the summer months. Suggest one reason for this.

4 There is an increasing tendency for several port authorities on one estuary to merge into one large port authority to control all these ports and make them more efficient. Can you see any evidence of this on the map?

Since Scotland has such a long coastline and many islands ports have always had an important role to play throughout history. As times have changed so have the ports. A study of the following model highlights some of these changes.

113

Models of an estuary port

Fig. 160(a), (b), (c), shows three stages in the development of a model port and the subsequent growth of a city. Although this port is imaginary it illustrates the main changes which many of Scotland's large ports have undergone.

Stage one — Fig. 160(a)
1. The first sign of port development began, when a bridge was built encouraging a small settlement called Estuary Port to grow as a **route centre**. All the main north-south routes used this bridge since it was the lowest bridge on the river.
2. As time passed **small wooden quays** were **built** and the settlement grew as a small **trading centre**. Many of the goods were transported by small rowing or wind-powered boats.
3. As trade increased, new longer **stone quays**

were built and **jetties** were extended out into the river. The river was deepened and straightened to allow more and larger boats to come up the river and dock at the port.

Stage two — Fig. 160(b)
By this time the **Industrial Revolution** was well under way — ships were now larger and powered by **steam**, materials were manufactured on a large scale and inland transport was greatly improved by the development of **canals** and **railways**. As a result the small settlement grew into a large industrial centre.

All these changes encouraged the growth of **trade** not only with other ports in the country, but with ports abroad; and so **Estuary Port** became more and more crowded with ships. Large **docks** (see Fig. 166) had to be built so that these ships could land their cargo at **Estuary Port**.

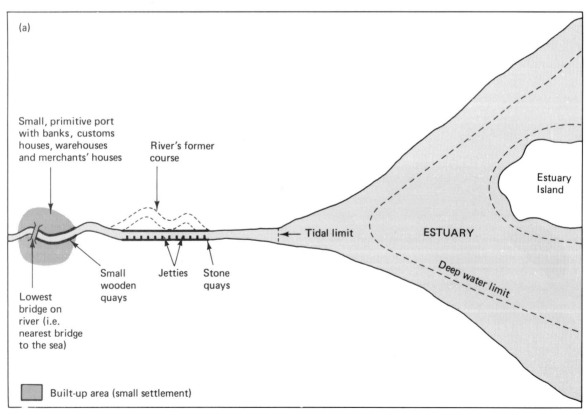

Fig. 160 a)   Estuary Port model stage one — before 19th Century

114

Stage three – Fig. 160(c)

The trend towards larger ships speeded up markedly in the 20th century and for the transport of some types of cargo the smaller vessels of earlier times have been replaced by huge ships in order to cut down building, fuel and labour costs. (One large oil tanker for example is more economic than three smaller ones carrying the same total load.) Such huge ships however need deeper and wider stretches of water, and so must be loaded and unloaded nearer to the open sea. Three completely new developments have taken place this century:

1. Container Terminals (Fig. 161)

This is simply a dock where metal **containers** of a standard size are used in the transport of cargo. Containers can be transferred from a ship to a container lorry or container train very easily with the use of a crane. They therefore have three main advantages:

(a) They save **time** because the goods inside the containers can be loaded and unloaded more quickly from ship to dock without being disturbed;

(b) They save **money** because less machinery is used to transport containers than would be necessary if the goods inside were transported individually. Also fewer workers are needed so less money is needed to pay wages.

(c) Containers protect the goods inside against the weather and mis-handling.

However containers have two major disadvantages:

(a) Since fewer workers are needed unemployment results;

(b) Container ports need very large dockside space for storage.

2. Specialised Quays (see Figs. 162 and 163)

These allow the handling of goods of one particular type in **large quantities**. The goods e.g. wheat, iron ore and oil are transported by special 'bulk carrier' ships which have equipment specialised for handling this cargo.

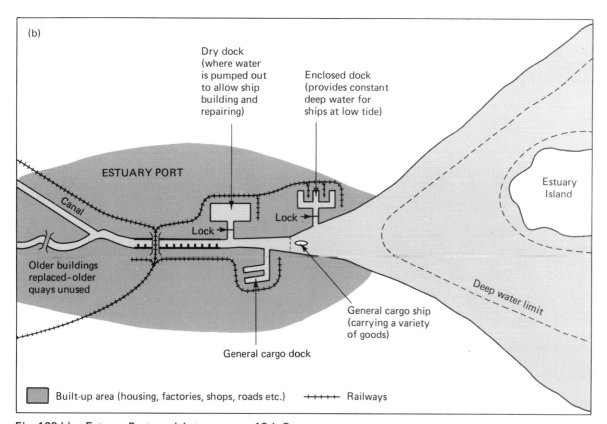

Fig. 160 b)   Estuary Port model stage two – 19th Century

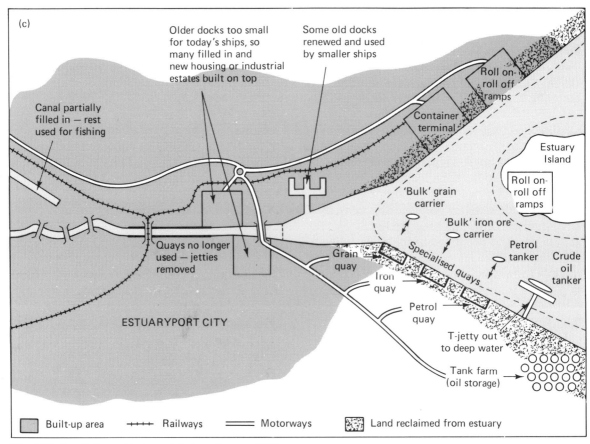

(c)

Older docks too small for today's ships, so many filled in and new housing or industrial estates built on top

Some old docks renewed and used by smaller ships

Roll on-roll off ramps

Container terminal

Canal partially filled in — rest used for fishing

Estuary Island

Roll on-roll off ramps

'Bulk' grain carrier

'Bulk' iron ore carrier

Petrol tanker

Crude oil tanker

Quays no longer used — jetties removed

Grain quay

Specialised quays

Iron quay

Petrol quay

T-jetty out to deep water

ESTUARYPORT CITY

Tank farm (oil storage)

| Built-up area | +++ Railways | Motorways | Land reclaimed from estuary |

Fig. 160 c)   Estuary Port model stage three — 20th Century

Fig. 162   Finnart oil terminal on Loch Long

Fig. 161   Greenock container terminal

Specialised cranes lift them off and drop them in specialised storage facilities e.g. some goods must be frozen and others kept dry etc. These ships, cranes and storage areas may be useless

Fig. 163   Hunterston ore and coal terminal, Ayrshire

for anything other than the handling of one particular cargo, e.g. an oil tank is useless for storing wheat, but like container facilities they are much more efficient and so save time and money.

3. Roll On/Roll Off Facilities (see Fig. 164)
As road transport gradually became more important than railway or canal transport, roll on/roll off facilities were developed i.e. ramps were built from the shore so that ships or ferries could lower a second ramp and allow industrial road vehicles to drive straight onto the ship without disturbing their freight. Motorists can now take their car across water barriers. These facilities are important to people travelling from **Estuary Port** to **Estuary Island**.

Fig. 164   Roll on/roll off facilities at Ardrossan

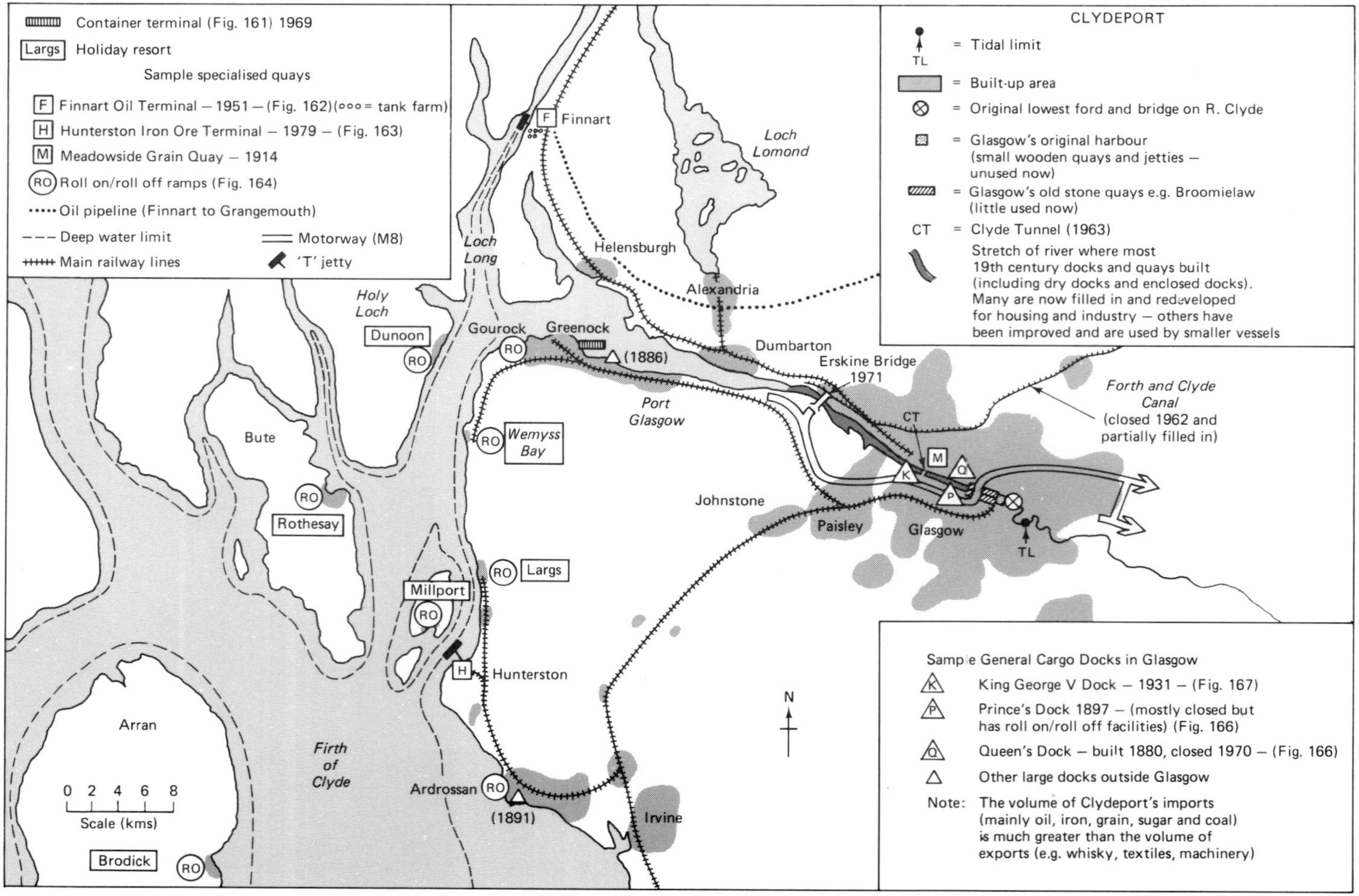
Container terminal (Fig. 161) 1969
Largs Holiday resort
Sample specialised quays
F Finnart Oil Terminal – 1951 – (Fig. 162)(ooo = tank farm)
H Hunterston Iron Ore Terminal – 1979 – (Fig. 163)
M Meadowside Grain Quay – 1914
RO Roll on/roll off ramps (Fig. 164)
Oil pipeline (Finnart to Grangemouth)
Deep water limit
Main railway lines
Motorway (M8)
'T' jetty
CLYDEPORT
TL = Tidal limit
= Built-up area
= Original lowest ford and bridge on R. Clyde
= Glasgow's original harbour (small wooden quays and jetties – unused now)
= Glasgow's old stone quays e.g. Broomielaw (little used now)
CT = Clyde Tunnel (1963)
Stretch of river where most 19th century docks and quays built (including dry docks and enclosed docks). Many are now filled in and redeveloped for housing and industry – others have been improved and are used by smaller vessels
Sample General Cargo Docks in Glasgow
K King George V Dock – 1931 – (Fig. 167)
P Prince's Dock 1897 – (mostly closed but has roll on/roll off facilities) (Fig. 166)
Q Queen's Dock – built 1880, closed 1970 – (Fig. 166)
Other large docks outside Glasgow
Note: The volume of Clydeport's imports (mainly oil, iron, grain, sugar and coal) is much greater than the volume of exports (e.g. whisky, textiles, machinery)
Finnart
Loch Lomond
Loch Long
Helensburgh
Alexandria
Holy Loch
Dunoon
Gourock
Greenock
(1886)
Dumbarton
Erskine Bridge 1971
Forth and Clyde Canal (closed 1962 and partially filled in)
Port Glasgow
Wemyss Bay
Bute
Rothesay
Johnstone
Paisley
Glasgow
Largs
Millport
Hunterston
Arran
Firth of Clyde
Ardrossan
(1891)
Irvine
N
0 2 4 6 8
Scale (kms)
Brodick

Fig. 165 Clydeport

Although **Estuary Port** is an imaginary or **model** port many real ports have developed in a similar way. We shall now look at such a port in Scotland i.e. **Clydeport**.

Clydeport

Clydeport is not a single port in itself. It is the name given to a **group** of ports lying on the deep, sheltered estuary of the Clyde between Glasgow and Ardrossan (Fig. 165).

The growth of Clydeport

<u>Before the 19th century.</u> Much of the trading carried out on the Clyde during the Middle Ages took place in Glasgow and although there were other small ports downstream a large proportion of the imports and exports passed through this settlement.

Although a few wooden quays were built to allow goods to be loaded and unloaded from small rowing boats, the development of a port at Glasgow was restricted by its west coast location and the shallowness of the river. This second problem encouraged the growth of ports in deeper water nearer the sea e.g. Irvine, Port Glasgow and (especially) Greenock.

By the late 18th century however, the Clyde had been deepened and straightened allowing larger boats to reach Glasgow, stone quays had been built along the Broomielaw downstream from the original harbour, and Glasgow had a flourishing trade with America. In addition the Forth and Clyde Canal had been built to allow larger vessels to reach the northern outskirts of the town. As a result Glasgow grew rapidly and became the main port on the Clyde once again.

<u>19th century.</u> To cope with the huge increase in trade during the Industrial Revolution several large general cargo docks (Fig. 166), dry docks and enclosed docks were built in Glasgow and Greenock. (Greenock however lost much of its trade to Glasgow when the Clyde was deepened even more.)

<u>20th century.</u> The great increase in size of ships this century has however caused new problems for Glasgow. Despite being deepened

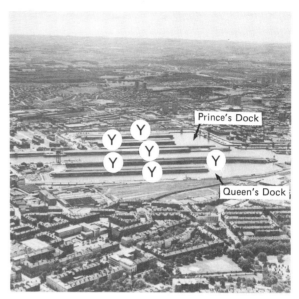

Fig. 166   Queen's Dock and Prince's Dock

and straightened, the River Clyde is far too narrow and shallow for many of the large ships of today to reach the city. As a result several of Glasgow's docks have closed down and most of the main port developments in the 20th century have been nearer the Clyde Estuary. These are shown on Fig. 165.

So that all these port developments (both old and new) can be used more efficiently they are now controlled by one authority — the Clydeport Authority — and each port will therefore develop in future as one section of a large port i.e. Clydeport.

Fig. 167   King George V Dock

119

Exercise

1 Explain is your own words what is meant by a 'port'.

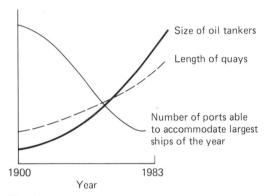

Fig. 168

2 Examine Fig. 168. Describe and try to explain the three trends shown on the graph.

3 (a) Suggest why a small port developed downstream from point X on Fig. 165.
(b) Name four types of building you would expect to see developing around this port in the 18th century.

4 (a) Suggest why Prince's Dock and Queen's Dock (Fig. 166) are much less important today than they were in the 19th century.
(b) Suggest the function of the buildings (labelled Y) on the dockside.

(c) Name one large dock in Glasgow which is still operating (see Fig. 167).
(d) Suggest a possible reason why this dock has survived while others have not.
(e) Explain what is meant by a general cargo dock.

5 (a) Explain what is meant by a specialised quay. Refer to Figs. 162 and 163 in your answer.
(b) Describe and explain the distribution of the specialised quays on Fig. 165.

6 (a) Which significant 20th century port development is found at Greenock? (See Fig. 161)
(b) What are the advantages and disadvantages of this type of development?

7 The landscape on either side of the Clyde is continually changing e.g. between Glasgow and Greenock there is much evidence of a declining industry, while further down from Greenock another industry is continuing to develop particularly in towns like Largs, Dunoon, Millport, Brodick and Rothesay.
(a) Using Fig. 165 suggest what these two industries might be.
(b) Explain the significance of roll on/roll off facilities to one of these industries.

8 Copy and complete Fig. 169 comparing Clydeport to the model, Estuary Port.

STAGE	SIMILARITIES		DIFFERENCES
Before 19th century	1	1	Many small harbours developed on the Clyde estuary — not only Glasgow (e.g. Greenock, Irvine and Port Glasgow)
	2	2	Glasgow's harbour was tidal
	3	3	
19th century	1	1	
	2	2	
20th century	1	1	
	2	2	
	3	3	

Fig. 169   Comparison of Clydeport with Estuary Port model

Airports

Advantages and disadvantages of air transport

Travel by aeroplane has one great advantage over the other three methods of transport already studied. Since the routes are influenced much less by surface barriers like mountains, estuaries or peninsulas, and since air provides less resistance to speed than water, railway tracks or road surfaces, air transport is on the whole much **faster** than rail, road or sea transport.

It is however more **expensive** and so only certain groups of passenger and freight usually travel by aeroplane in Scotland. These include:
Freight (a) Goods which are of **high value** but small in size and **weight** — since the cost of their transport will only be a small proportion of their value e.g. computer components.
(b) Perishable goods i.e. goods which need to be transported quickly before they are destroyed or lose their value e.g. fruit, flowers (and newspapers).
Passengers (a) People who are ill and are far away from hospitals e.g. in Western Isles.
(b) Businessmen to whom cost is less important than time. (c) People going on holiday abroad.

Like other forms of transport air travel is greatly influenced by the weather e.g. pilots must try to land and take off into the wind as winds blowing across the runways can cause difficulties. The element of weather which provides most worries for pilots is **fog**, since even today, except in some specially equipped planes, the pilots rely on their eyes to fly the aeroplane safely. Both fog and high crosswinds can cause airports to shut down temporarily and this can cause great delays. More and more airports are however being equipped with highly sophisticated landing aids and so fog is becoming less of a problem all the time.

Exercise

1 The location of an airport
An airport cannot be built anywhere. Many different factors both physical and human must be examined. In Fig. 170 column A lists the main features which a site must have if an airport is to be located there. Copy the table and complete column B by explaining why each feature is so important to the site of an airport.

A	B
1. Near to a large town or city	
2. Good road and rail links to the city	
3. Flat, well drained stable land	
4. An area relatively free from weather hazards, especially fog	

Fig. 170

2 'Even if a site with the four characteristics above is found, the construction of an airport may still not be carried out because of protests by people living in the local area.' Discuss this statement with your teacher then in at least 50 words state which people may object to the construction of an airport and explain why they would object.
Clues: there are two types of complaint — one type against the airport itself and the other against the aircraft.

3 A 'model' site for an airport
(a) Examine the imaginary region shown in Fig. 171. Imagine you have been provided with a number of possible sites for the location of an airport (A–E). Copy Fig. 172 and complete it by adding a tick if the site has the advantage listed. Add up the ticks for each site and then decide which site would be the best for the construction of a new airport.
(b) Write a sentence to summarise the reasons why you would locate your airport on this site.
(c) Can you think of any problems caused by locating your airport here?

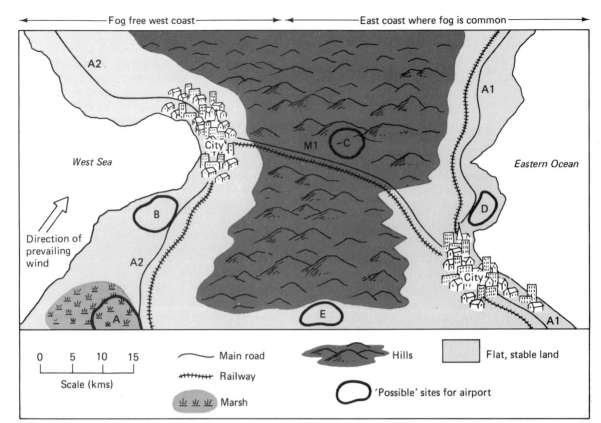

Fig. 171

Site	Within 15 kms of city	Good road + rail links	Flat stable land	Fog free	Total ticks
A					
B					
C					
D					
E					

Fig. 172

4 Examine Fig. 173 showing the main airports and air routes in Scotland.

(a) Explain the difference between an **airport** and an **airstrip**.

(b) Explain why Aberdeen, Glasgow, Edinburgh and Prestwick have much larger airports than the others.

(c) Suggest two reasons why, despite their small size, the airports, airstrips, and heliports found in the Highlands and Islands are extremely important to the people living there.

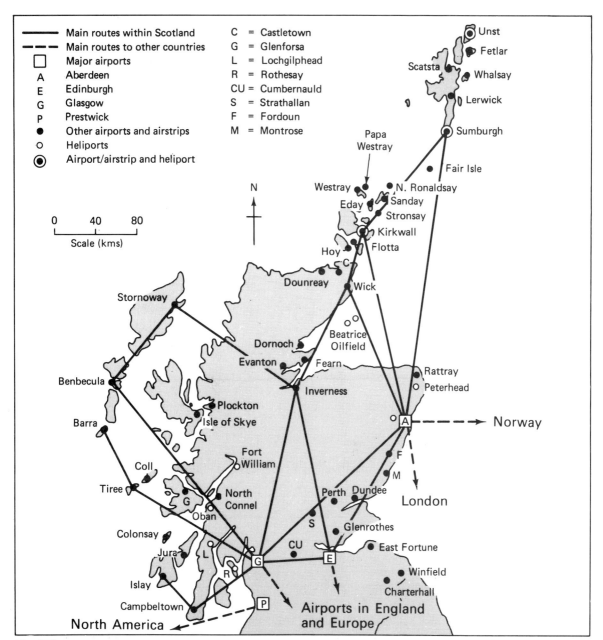

Fig. 173   Air transport in Scotland

Glasgow Airport

Glasgow Airport, Scotland's newest and busiest passenger airport, was developed in 1966 to replace the smaller Renfrew Airport which had no more room for expansion. Although dealing with freight to and from Europe, the main cargo is passengers, e.g. holiday makers flying to and from Europe, businessmen being shuttled to London or Western Islanders flying home.

Exercise

1 One problem with the site of Glasgow Airport was that much of the land was unstable and had to be improved, but the advantages possessed by this location far outweighed this problem. Examine the map showing the situation of Glasgow Airport (Fig. 174) and explain why it was an excellent situation for the construction of an airport.

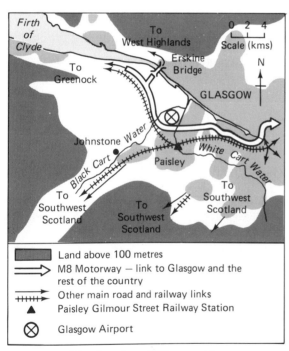

Fig. 174   The situation of Glasgow Airport

2 Many people argue that Glasgow Airport was built on 'the wrong side of the city'. Referring to the distribution of population in Central Scotland try to explain this view.

3 The airport authorities have provided 'home improvement' grants for many people living under the flight path of jets using Glasgow Airport.
   (a) Suggest what type of 'home improvements' might be covered by these grants.
   (b) Explain why they are necessary.

4 Glasgow Airport is now fairly accessible to Cumbernauld, Irvine and East Kilbride. Explain why this is of particular importance to these towns.

5 Examine the map of Glasgow Airport itself (Fig. 175).
   (a) Between which two compass directions does the main runway lie?
   (b) Explain why it has been built this way.
   (c) Why do you think there is a smaller runway aligned in a completely different direction?

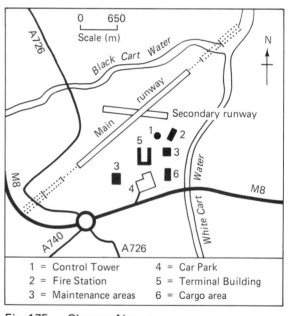

Fig. 175   Glasgow Airport

6 (a) What features do you think are represented by the dots (···|:::) on the map?
   (b) Explain their importance.
   (c) The main runway is 2566 metres long. Explain why such a long runway is necessary today.
   (d) Why does the airport have its own fire station?

7 Pilots landing or taking off at Glasgow, or any other airport must always have a detailed weather report. Explain why this is so important in at least 30 words.

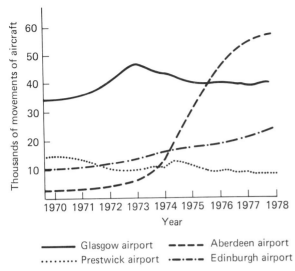

Fig. 176   Air transport movements 1970–1978

Legend:
——— Glasgow airport   – – – Aberdeen airport
········· Prestwick airport   ·—·—·— Edinburgh airport

8 Examine Fig. 176.
(a) Name the only airport which has not shown an increase in air transport movements since 1970.
(b) Which airport has shown the most marked increase, especially since 1972?
(c) Suggest an explanation for your answer to (b).

Electricity supplies

Electricity is one of the safest, cleanest and most convenient forms of energy available to us today. It has an enormous variety of uses in factories, homes and offices throughout the country. But where does the massive amount of electrical energy (electricity) come from? Today it is produced in **power stations** using running water, uranium or fossil fuels (such as coal, oil or gas which have been formed from the remains of dead organisms), as shown in Fig. 177.

The electricity produced is fed into the **National Grid**, a network of overhead lines and underground cables, covering the whole country. In this way, surplus power in one part of the country can be channelled to areas where there is a shortage of power. Since electricity cannot be stored this transfer of power from one place to another reduces wastage. Before reaching the factory, home or other consumer the electricity must be reduced in power by **transformers**. Fig. 178 shows the main power stations and high voltage transmission lines (**supergrid**) in Scotland.

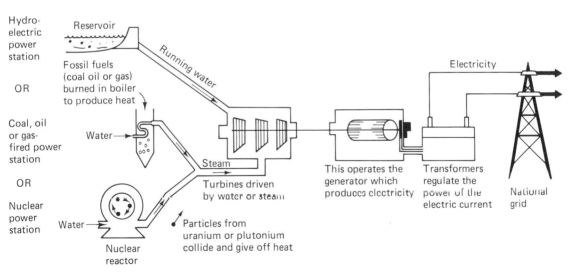

Fig. 177   Making electricity

The location of power stations

Since electricity can be transmitted efficiently over long distances by high voltage cables or lines the larger power stations do not need to be very near to the consumer. They can therefore be located on sites where they can be most efficiently supplied with **fuel**.

Hydroelectric power stations

In a **hydroelectric** power station **running water** is used to drive **turbines** which operate **generators** which in turn produce electricity. As Fig. 178 shows most H.E.P. stations in Scotland are found in the central and western Highlands. There the high annual rainfall ensures supplies of water, the deep valleys allow it to be easily stored and the hard impermeable rocks provide a firm foundation for dams and prevent leakage of water. (A study of these power stations can be found in Chapter 8.)

All other types of station shown in Fig. 178 use a fuel to produce heat for converting water into steam which is then used to drive the turbines. They all lie on flat, stable land (capable of holding heavy buildings) near the coast (since they need large supplies of water for cooling purposes).

Oil fired stations

These burn oil to produce heat and need to be near deep water harbours so that tankers can supply them efficiently with oil.

Coal fired stations

These stations burn coal to produce the necessary heat and are all found on coalfields on sites with good railway links so that coal can be brought in efficiently.

Gas turbine stations

These burn gas to produce heat and they are located near to the terminals of North Sea crude oil pipelines, so that they can use the gas which is separated from the oil. There is one such station at Dunfermline.

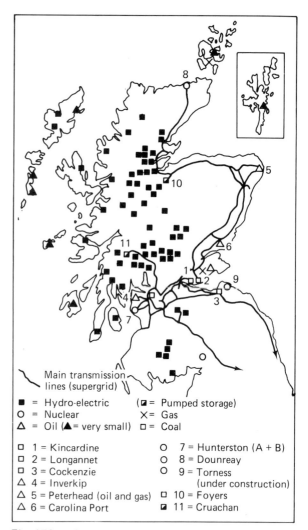

Fig. 178   Scotland's 'supergrid' and power stations

Nuclear power stations

In nuclear power stations the necessary heat is produced by the controlled fission (splitting) of **uranium** atoms in a building called a reactor. Although they are expensive to build nuclear power stations can generate electricity more cheaply than coal or oil fired stations. Very little fuel is needed (one tonne of uranium can be made to release as much heat as 20 000 tonnes of coal) and most experts believe that nuclear power will take over as our major source of energy in the future as coal, oil and gas become more and more expensive to extract and (eventually) run out.

One problem with nuclear power is that the splitting of atoms releases **radiation** which, if allowed to escape, would present a serious threat to living things in the surrounding area. Strict precautions must therefore be taken to ensure that no radiation leakage occurs and that the radioactive waste products are disposed of safely.

Nuclear power stations tend to be located on sites well away from highly populated areas so that if the worst did happen the area could be quickly evacuated.

Exercise

1 Explain the meaning of the following terms in your own words: **power station; fossil fuel; hydroelectric power; national grid.**

2 (a) Describe and explain the effect the development of electric power has had on the **distribution** of industry in Scotland.
(b) In some parts of the country electricity pylons are not permitted. Suggest a reason for this and possible alternatives.

3 Examine the photograph of Longannet power station (Fig. 100 on p. 73).
(a) Which fuel does this power station use? (See Fig. 97 on p. 70)
(b) Describe and explain the location of this power station.
(c) Suggest why the chimney must be so tall.
(d) Describe in at least 60 words what is happening inside this power station (use Fig. 177 to help you).

4 Examine Fig. 179 carefully.
(a) Describe how the importance of nuclear fuel as a source of electricity is expected to change.
(b) Explain you answer to (a).
(c) Despite the need for the development of nuclear power stations many people strongly object to their construction. What do you think their reasons are?

5 Fig. 179 shows that 'other' newer sources of power (which are today only at very experimental stages) may produce more of our electricity in the future. Try to find out what some of these 'other' sources of power may be.

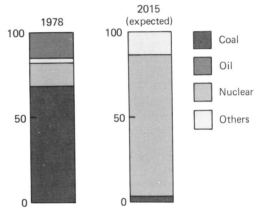

Fig. 179   Sources of UK electricity in 1978 and 2015 (%)

8
Highland landscapes

The Highlands (and Islands) of Scotland

Using an atlas copy and complete the key in Fig. 180.

The area of land north of the fault running from Stonehaven to Helensburgh is referred to as the **Scottish Highlands (and Islands)**. This area has the highest, most rugged, barren, but perhaps most beautiful landscape in the country, and although it covers over 60% of Scotland's area it is the least densely populated of Scotland's three sections.

Relief

Millions of years ago the ancient Highland rocks formed a high plateau which tilted from west to east, as shown in Fig. 181, but since then the plateau has been greatly altered by natural processes like faulting, volcanic activity, weathering and erosion. The plateau is now much lower than it was and has been broken up into several blocks separated by deep steep-sided valleys (see Figs. 182 and 183) carved out by river and glacial erosion.

River erosion

Water falling as rain on the plateau became channelled into rivers which worked their way to the sea following fault lines and other lines of weakness, wearing away the rocks and carving up the plateau into blocks separated by V-shaped river valleys. As a result of the west-east tilt of the Highlands the rivers flowing westwards tend to be short and fast-flowing, carving deeper valleys, those flowing to the east tend to be longer and more slowly flowing.

Glaciation

In the Highlands however, most of the river valleys lost their V-shape thousands of years ago when the temperatures dropped to well below what they are today and much of the land was covered in great masses of ice. Fig. 185 (a, b and c) shows how the Highland

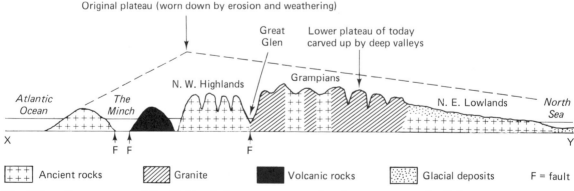

Fig. 181   Cross-section of the Highlands from west to east showing structure and relief

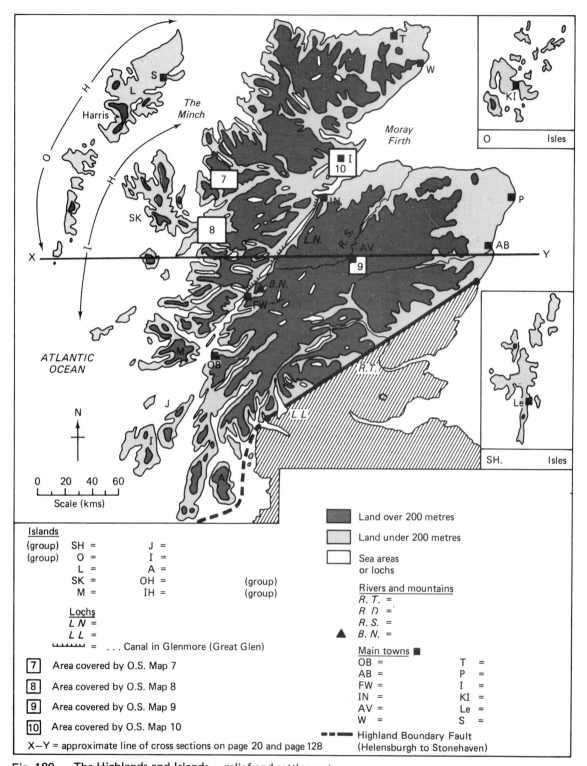

Fig. 180   The Highlands and Islands — relief and settlement

Fig. 182   The dissected plateau of the Highlands

valleys were altered during this 'Ice Age'. Snow falling into valleys or hollows accumulated to such depths that the weight of the snow in the top layers caused the snow underneath to turn to ice. Gradually great 'rivers of ice' called **glaciers** were formed. These glaciers moved around in the hollows deepening them by erosion into **corries** (or **coires** on O.S. maps) i.e. bowl-shaped features with steep back and side walls. When the ice melted deep lakes or **lochans** were left in many of these corries, some with small streams flowing over the **lip** (or lower side) of the corrie and falling into the valleys below (see Fig. 184). Where two corries developed side by side the mountainside between them was eroded to form sharp-edged ridges called

aretes and where corries developed all around a mountain all that often remained were jagged **pyramidal peaks**. As snow continued to fall, glaciers flowed out of the corries 'bulldozing' their way along river valleys and **truncating** any **spurs** in their path i.e. cutting the ends off any pieces of land sticking out into the valleys. They deepened, straightened and widened the valleys changing them from a V-shape into a U-shape. The rocks along the floors of the valleys were picked up and carried along with other rocks falling from surrounding slopes then deposited when the glaciers melted further down the valleys on surrounding lowlands or in the sea. Any material carried and deposited by glaciers is known as **moraine**.

Fig. 183   A U-shaped valley

When temperatures rose again the glaciers began to retreat back up the valleys and moraine was deposited along the valley bottoms. Many inland lakes or **lochs** were formed where these deposits dammed rivers.

Today lochs can also be found in basins cut out by glaciers in parts of the valleys where rocks were softer and more easily eroded or where the glaciers became more powerful due to ice being added from corries or tributary valleys. These tributary valleys usually contained smaller, less powerful glaciers and as a result they were not cut so deeply. When the ice melted in these valleys they were left as **hanging valleys** with the tributaries tumbling over waterfalls into the main valley and depositing material at the bottom forming features called **alluvial fans**.

Fig. 184   A corrie

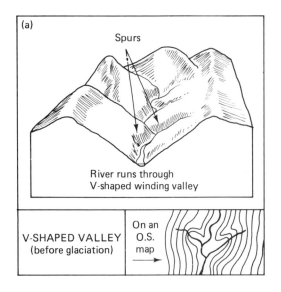

(a)

Spurs

River runs through
V-shaped winding valley

V-SHAPED VALLEY (before glaciation)	On an O.S. map →

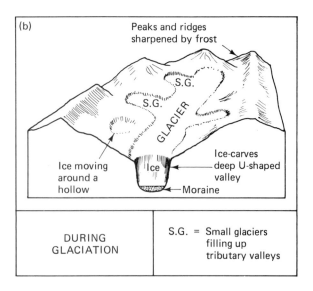

(b)

Peaks and ridges
sharpened by frost

S.G.
S.G.
GLACIER

Ice moving
around a
hollow

Ice

Ice-carves
deep U-shaped
valley

Moraine

DURING GLACIATION	S.G. = Small glaciers filling up tributary valleys

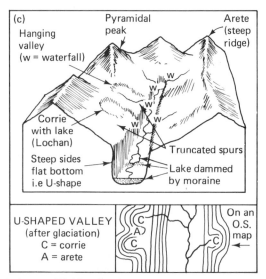

(c)

Pyramidal
peak

Arete
(steep
ridge)

Hanging
valley
(w = waterfall)

w
w
w
w
w
w

Corrie
with lake
(Lochan)

Truncated spurs

Steep sides
flat bottom
i.e U-shape

Lake dammed
by moraine

U-SHAPED VALLEY (after glaciation) C = corrie A = arete	On an O.S. map ←

Fig. 185   The affects of glaciation on Highland valleys

Around the coast (particularly in the west) many of the U-shaped valleys were cut so deeply that their floors lay below sea level. When the ice melted the sea flooded these valleys forming deep **fjords**.

Also found around the coasts are narrow bands of flat land known as **raised beaches**. Fig. 186 shows how these have been formed.

During times of less severe glaciation many ridges and peaks stood out above the ice as shown in Fig. 185. At such times they were sharpened by **frost action** – a process which continues today and involves water seeping into cracks, freezing, expanding and shattering the rocks into sharp edged fragments or **scree**. An examination of Fig. 182 however shows that many of the mountains in the Highlands have rounded summits. This suggests that they were completely covered in ice at least some of the time and that the ice smoothed off their tops.

Now that most of the ice has gone rivers have again become the main agents of erosion. Those flowing along U-shaped valleys are often called misfit rivers since they are far narrower than the valley bottoms.

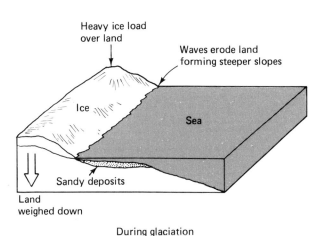 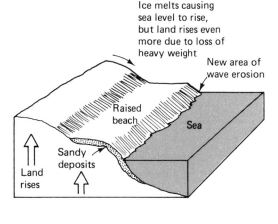

During glaciation   After glaciation

Fig. 186   Formation of a raised beach

It is important to remember that there are large areas of low land within the Highlands e.g. along the North Sea coast, around the Moray Firth, in Caithness and on many of the Islands.

Climate

Due mainly to the area's high latitude and high altitude the Highlands and Islands generally have lower temperatures more rain and more snow than other parts of the U.K. The area is however very large and so there are variations of climate within it. These variations are described on pages 19 to 22.

Soils and land use

Most of the Central and Western Highlands consist of wild wet mountainside made of old, hard impermeable rock worn down by ice. Soils here are thin, acidic, stoney and infertile and often contain large amounts of **peat** (a brown/black substance consisting of dead plant material which has only partly decayed due to the waterlogged, airless conditions in the soil) particularly where slopes are more gentle.

Today these soils support unimproved moorland of heather, coarse grass or bracken used mainly for the rough grazing of sheep or as **deer forest** i.e. areas kept clear of trees for the hunting of deer. Large tracts of these moorlands have been bought over by the Forestry Commission for the planting of trees.

The only places suitable for cultivation are the raised beaches or valley bottoms where glacial and alluvial (river) deposits provide deeper soils. In these areas, hill sheep farmers or crofters have improved the soils by draining them and adding lime and fertilizer so that winter fodder can be grown.

Soils in the lowlands around the east coast are of much higher quality. Many are based on much younger, softer rocks while others have developed from glacial or alluvial deposits and they have been greatly improved by generations of people. Here the main land uses are arable farming and the rearing and feeding of livestock like sheep and beef cattle.

Exercise

Examination of a typical highland landscape
The area around Upper Loch Torridon (area 7 on Fig. 180) illustrates many features common throughout the western Highlands. Examine O.S. Map 7 and answer the following questions:

1 The photo (Fig. 187) shows a view of the area around upper Loch Torridon. Write a short description of the landscape shown. (Your answer should refer to relief and land use in particular).

133

Fig. 187　　Upper Loch Torridon

2　(a) Copy and complete the slope analysis table
below (Fig. 188): (The numbers are found by
counting the contours crossing the easting on the
left-hand side of the square.)

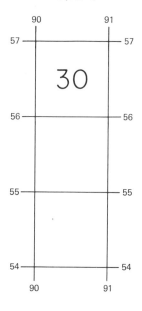

Fig. 188

(b) Copy and complete the cross-section across
Glen Torridon (Fig. 189).

(c) Analyse your completed diagrams and copy
and complete the paragraph below:
'The cross-section and slope analysis table indicate
that Glen Torridon is a _____ shaped valley. This
would suggest that it has been shaped by the work
of a _____ . If Glen Torridon was a normal river
valley its cross-section would have been _____
shaped.

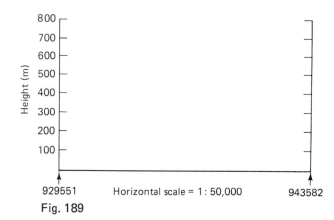

Fig. 189

134

3 Examine the feature in the area shown in Fig. 190 (Loch Coire an Ruadh-Staic). It shows a small, almost flat area with steep slopes leading upwards on three sides. Draw a section along the line a–b:

(a) What name is given to this type of feature?

(b) How is it formed?

(c) Explain why it contains a small Lake (Lochan).

(d) Give two pieces of evidence **from the map** which suggest that the sides or walls of this feature are very steep.

(e) What do you think the arrows on the sketch illustrate?

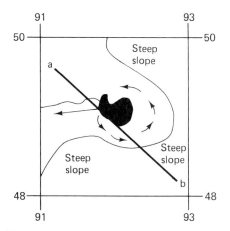

Fig. 190

4 (a) Fig. 191 shows a long profile of the flow of water from Loch an Turaraich (885 491) to the jetty on the shore of Upper Loch Torridon at 847 548. Copy and complete the diagram by writing in the following features above the correct arrows;

Upper Loch Torridon, Jetties, Tiny Lochan

(unnamed), Loch Damh, Footbridge, Falls of Balgy, A896.

(b) The area around Loch an Turaraich (8849) could be described as a miniature version of which typical glacial feature?

(c) Suggest how the valley containing Loch Damh was formed.

(d) Suggest why Loch Damh is at its deepest at point X (your answer should refer to Loch an Turaraich).

(e) (i) is Upper Loch Torridon a sea loch (fjord) or an inland loch?

(ii) Give two pieces of map evidence to support your answer.

(iii) Explain how Upper Loch Torridon was formed.

5 Copy and complete the table, Fig. 192, using examples which have not already been mentioned in this exercise.

6 'Now that temperatures are much higher than they were during the great ice-ages, running water has again become the main valley forming instrument.' Using four-figure grid references give examples of rivers which are cutting their own valleys without the help of glaciers.

7 Using your answers to questions 1–6 write a paragraph of at least 100 words describing the relief and drainage of the area covered by O.S. Map 7.

8 (a) Describe and explain the distribution of **settlements** in this area.

(b) (i) Copy and complete the topological map, Fig. 193, using the **Beta Index** and decide whether the settlements around Upper Loch Torridon are well connected or not. (You may want to refer to p. 108.)

(ii) Explain your answer.

Note: draw the roads in red so that you do not

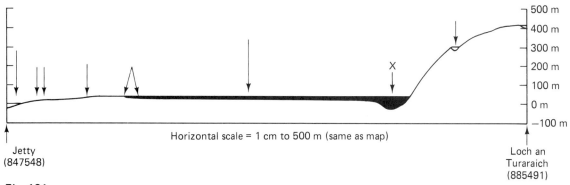

Horizontal scale = 1 cm to 500 m (same as map)

Jetty
(847548)

Loch an
Turaraich
(885491)

Fig. 191

Glacial feature	Name and 4 figure grid references of two examples	
Corrie	1.	2.
U-shaped valley	1.	2.
Inland loch ('ribbon' loch)	1.	2.
Sea loch (Fjord)	1.	2.

Fig. 192

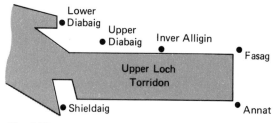

Fig. 193

confuse them with the coastline.
(c) The actual road distance between Shieldaig and Lower Diabaig is 26 km. Using the map and the **Detour Index** decide whether or not this is an efficient route. (You may want to refer to p. 110.)
(d) Suggest how this route could be made more efficient.
(e) Explain why it is unlikely that this will happen in the near future.
(f) The land-use in this area is obviously limited due to the physical landscape, but these limitations may **encourage** certain types of land-use or activity. Copy and complete the following table Fig. 194 by adding the land-use which is suggested by the symbols at each grid reference.
(g) The O.S. Map shows that the woodlands are restricted to certain areas.
   (i) Describe and explain the distribution of these wooded areas.
   (ii) Why is it that other large areas of the map

Grid reference	Activity
848577	
888543	
877570	

Fig. 194

are described as forest e.g. Torridon Forest (9159) when they have few (if any) trees growing in them?

Traditional Highland occupations

Although many 'new' industries have been introduced to the Highlands in recent years a large percentage of the population still work in occupations which have employed people for many decades. Three of these 'traditional occupations' are fishing, crofting and whisky distilling.

Fishing

The North Sea and the waters around the Hebrides are shallow enough to allow light to reach the sea bed. This encourages the growth of plant life which provides food for millions of fish. As a result many Highlanders have obtained at least part of their income from fishing for many years. Fig. 195 shows the main fishing ports in the Highlands.

Basically there are four main types of catch in Scottish waters:
1. Surface swimmers e.g. herring, mackerel, which as the name suggests live near the surface of the sea.
2. Deep water fish, e.g. white fish like cod and haddock.
3. Shellfish e.g. lobster, prawns or crabs. These have become more important as tastes have changed and living standards have improved in recent years.
4. Freshwater fish e.g. salmon and trout, which are caught in inland lochs and rivers

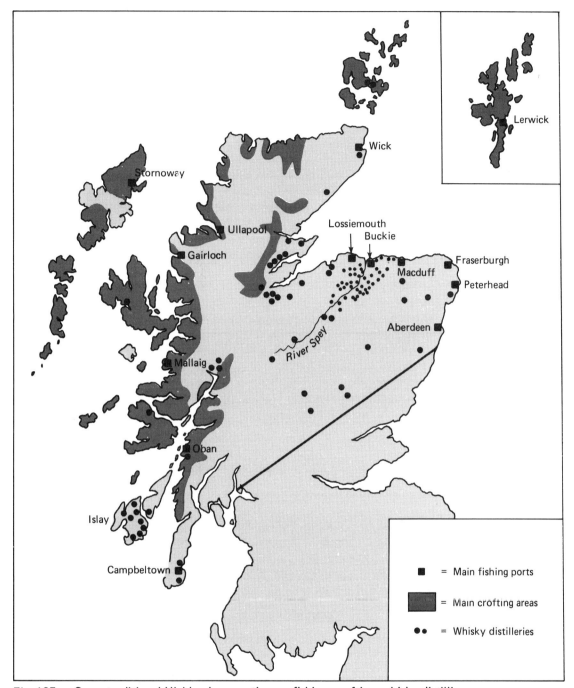

Fig. 195   Some traditional Highland occupations — fishing, crofting, whisky distilling

(especially those flowing into the North Sea) for industry or sport. Many of these are caught by anglers who pay for a licence to fish.

The fishing industry not only employs 6000 highlanders directly but also provides the basis for other industries in many of the ports e.g. fish processing (freezing, canning,

Fig. 196   Fishing port of Mallaig

smoking) making fertilizers and fish meal (for animals), boat building and repairing and net making.

Like all other industries, fishing is continually changing as new methods are applied. Most boats are now diesel powered, 'fish farms' are being developed where the fish are bred and reared in tanks and given the best conditions needed for growth, and some vessels are equipped with radar or echo-sounders which help locate the largest shoals of fish. The fishing industry, however, is not without its problems:

1. Many of the fishing grounds have been overfished and some fish, like the herring have been severely reduced in number. As a result herring fishing in Scottish waters was banned for a time to give the herring population a chance to recover.

2. In the 1970s many countries (like Canada and Iceland) extended their fishing grounds with the result that their fishermen are now able to sell fish more cheaply than British fishermen — even to Britain herself! Faced with this loss in market many fishermen in this country had to give up altogether.

3. When the United Kingdom joined the E.E.C. it was agreed that the fishing grounds around the coasts of all member countries should be shared amongst fishermen from each country. The United Kingdom's fishing grounds contain far more fish than those of the other countries and so British fishermen lost millions of pounds worth of fish to foreign fishermen. In 1983 however a new agreement was made that British fishermen should be allowed 37.3% of all the fish caught in E.E.C. waters, that the E.E.C. should continue to control the amount of fish being caught (to avoid overfishing) and that other countries should not be allowed to 'invade' Britain's most profitable fishing grounds. The agreement also made available a fund of millions of pounds to help all E.E.C. fishermen re-structure their fleets. It is hoped that such measures may lead to the recovery of the industry in Britain.

4. Even if such recovery does take place unemployment amongst British fishermen looks likely to increase since many of the smaller inefficient boats will have to be abandoned to make way for newer, more mechanised boats which need fewer men.

Exercise

1 Explain in your own words why the waters around the Highlands have provided extremely rich fishing grounds.

2 Name at least five other industries which may grow up in a port with a fishing fleet.

3 (a) Examine Figs. 146 and 148 on p. 104 and p. 105 showing Scotland's road and rail network. Which ports, those on the west or those on the east coast, are better served by communications?
(b) Explain why this is so important to the fishing industry.
(c) Most shellfish are sent live in special storage tanks to large cities by air and rail. Suggest reasons why shellfish are kept alive when it would be much easier and cheaper to transport dead fish.

4 Explain the importance of **fish-farms** and **echo-sounders** to the fishing industry today.

5 (a) Give three reasons why the fishing industry in Britain has suffered a severe decline in recent years.
(b) Describe some of the steps taken to halt or even reverse this decline.

Crofting

Crofting is a special way of life carried out by approximately 15 000 people living in the Scottish Islands and lowlying areas of the Northwest Highlands. Crofting is a type of

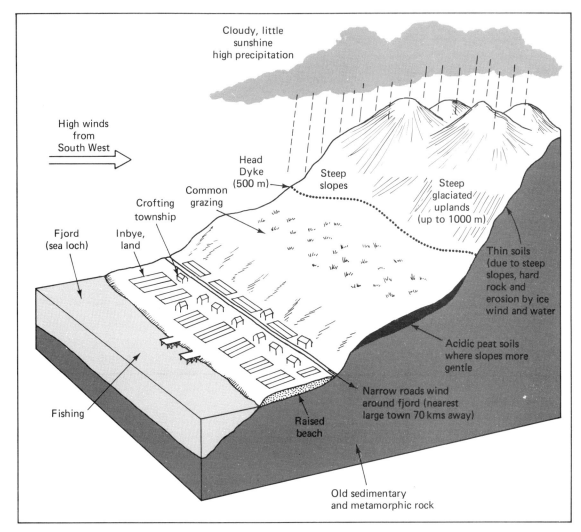

Fig. 197   A typical crofting landscape

farming, which, because of poor conditions (see Fig. 197) is usually carried out on a **part-time** basis. Crofters need a second occupation in order to make a decent living.

Farming on a croft is based mainly on the rearing of **livestock** (sheep and cattle) and the growing of crops in summer to feed these animals in winter. Most of the livestock is sold at local markets during the autumn sales when farmers from elsewhere in Scotland arrive to buy cattle and sheep for fattening on lowland farms.

Most crofts are found either along valley floors, or on coastal lowlands (often on sandy raised beaches as shown in Fig. 197) with the houses grouped together along a road into little **townships.**

In these crofting townships each crofter has the right to farm on two areas:
(a) Each crofter has a small area of land (the **inbye**) which is privately cultivated and usually lies near to the house. Here, hardy crops like oats, turnips and potatoes can be grown in summer in rotation with hay. The inbye is often fertilized with seaweed or cattle manure in addition to artificial fertilizers. Those crofters whose inbye land lies on a raised beach have the added

139

Fig. 198   A crofting township

advantage of light sandy soil which is easy to plough and contains shells which help to reduce the acidity of the soil.

(b) In summer animals are grazed on a larger area of **common grazing** land which is shared with all the other crofters in the township. The common grazing land can be on the lower slopes but often stretches well up the hillsides. In winter the animals are kept in the more sheltered inbye and fed on the crops grown there during the summer.

In each township much of the equipment like tractors and hand tools is shared and the crofters help one another with work like seeding, ploughing and harvesting (see Fig. 200). As a result there is a great community spirit in each little township — a very valuable asset in such a harsh environment.

Other occupations of crofters include the weaving of tweed cloth, forestry work, road work, postal work, driving and boat building/repairing. Many crofters in the past were also fishermen, but fishing has become increasingly a full-time occupation. Tourism is a growing industry which provides employment for crofters e.g. many people now work in shops and hotels while others offer bed and breakfast accommodation.

The Crofters' Commission

For many years now the number of crofters in the Scottish Highlands has been steadily decreasing as large numbers of people (particularly the young) have left in search of better opportunities elsewhere (see also pages 153–156). The remaining crofting population is

Fig. 199   A crofter cutting peat

now increasingly dominated by elderly people and there is a real danger that crofting could virtually die out as a way of life before very long. In an attempt to prevent this happening the government set up a special **Crofters' Commission** in 1955. The Commission can help crofters in a number of ways e.g. by providing **loans** for buying livestock or **grants** for the drainage of fields, the construction of fences and the reclamation of land from heather moor.

Despite the help and encouragement from the Crofters' Commission, however, the number of crofters in Scotland continues to drop. Only time will tell whether the Commission will eventually be successful or whether this traditional way of life will disappear altogether.

Fig. 200   Crofters harvesting potatoes

Exercise

1 'Crofting is a way of life which involves making the best living you can out of a very hostile physical environment.'

(a) Examine the sketch of a typical crofting landscape, Fig. 197, and describe the features of this environment which makes it so hostile. You should use the headings — **Relief, Climate, Soil** and **Isolation**.

(b) Despite all these problems, this landscape provides one physical feature which allows at least some cultivation to take place.

(i) Suggest what this landscape feature may be;
(ii) Explain how it was formed;
(iii) Explain why it provides better conditions for cultivation.

(c) Explain the meaning of the following terms in your own words: **livestock, inbye land, common grazing.** (Your answers for the last two should each be at least 30 words long.)

(d) Explain in at least 50 words why crofting is 'more a way of life than just a type of farming'.

2 Suggest two reasons why croft buildings are grouped together into small townships and not spread randomly over the landscape. (See Fig. 198.)

3 Crofters lead a very different life from most other Scottish people. Indeed many do not even speak English, but use another language.

(a) Find out what this language is called.
(b) Suggest why this language has survived in the crofting areas and has not been replaced by English.

4 Fig. 199 show a crofter cutting peat in summer. Suggest what it is used for (**Clue** — peat is a substance formed early in the formation of coal).

5 (a) Explain why the Crofters' Commission was set up.
(b) Give two ways in which the Commission can be of help to crofters.

Scotch whisky distilling

Making whisky
There are two types of Scotch whisky, i.e. **malt** (made from barley and water) and **grain** whisky (made from barley, maize and water). Most of the whisky made in the Highlands is **malt whisky,** made in buildings called **distilleries.** In a malt whisky distillery, specially prepared (malted) barley is dried

using **peat** and then mixed with hot water to produce a sugary liquid. Yeast is then added to convert this liquid into crude alcohol. The alcohol is then heated twice in huge copper **stills** (see Fig. 201) to remove impurities and produce vapourised alcohol which rises up the stills and is led off to be cooled into liquid spirit.

The spirit is emptied into large oak wood casks (see Fig. 202) where it is left for anything from three to fifteen years (sometimes even longer). Here the harsher constituents of the spirit evaporate through the wood and it matures into a mellow whisky — much of its golden colour is obtained from these casks.

When mature the whisky is usually transported to the Central Lowlands where it is **blended** with as many as fifty other whiskys, all produced in different parts of Scotland and all having a different flavour. It is then reduced in strength by water to form the most popular whiskys of today.

Location of distilleries
As Fig. 195 on p. 137 shows, whisky distilleries are found in many parts of the Highlands. A large proportion have however grown up in two areas in particular i.e. on the island of **Islay** and on **Speyside** (around the River Spey) where local farms provided barley and had a ready supply of peat and where **soft** water flowed in streams from surrounding hills. These advantages are still very important today and although some of the barley needed to supply Highland distilleries is transported north from England it is likely that the industry will remain in the Highlands for a very long time, especially now that many Highlanders have become highly skilled in whisky distilling.

A unique spirit
Scotch whisky cannot be imitated successfully anywhere in the world — the reasons for this are unknown but are thought to include the soft Scottish water, substances

Fig. 201   Stills in a Highland distillery

from the peat used for drying the barley, the effect of the Highland climate on the whisky as it matures in the casks, and the skill of the workers. Whatever the reason its distinctiveness is recognised by law and only whisky which has been distilled and matured in Scotland can be labelled 'Scotch Whisky'. Today over 80% of Scotch is exported and it is Scotland's most consistently successful export, bringing over £746 million into the country in 1980.

Exercise

1 Examine Figs. 201 and 202 and describe what is happening in each in at least 30 words.

2 Although whisky distilleries are found in many parts of the Highlands about half of them are concentrated in one area. Examine Fig. 31 on p. 25 and Fig. 195 on p. 137 then:
    (a) Name this area:
    (b) Suggest at least three reasons why so many distilleries grew up here.

3 Find out what is meant by 'soft' water;

4 'The whisky industry produces Scotland's second largest export and continues to make an important contribution to this country's balance of payments'; Explain what is meant by 'balance of payments';

5 (a) Several other countries have tried to imitate the flavour of Scotch whisky but without success. Suggest some reasons for this.
    (b) Suggest how Highlanders might be affected if these countries were successful.

Forestry in the Highlands

Hundreds of years ago much of the Highlands was covered in Scots pine, birch and oak trees, but since then most of the natural forest has been cleared to provide wood for fuel and building material and to clear the land for farming or urban land use. As a result of such massive clearance all over Britain the country became almost entirely dependent on imported wood.

Fig. 202   Wooden whisky casks in a Highland distillery

The problems of such a situation were brought home to the government when, during the First World War, most of these imports were cut off. This resulted in the Forestry Commission being set up in 1919 to purchase suitable land throughout the country for planting trees — in particular the quick-growing **softwood** trees like Scots pine, spruce and larch (some of which are exotic i.e. do not grow naturally in this part of Europe). Fortunately such trees grow in the harsh climate and poor thin soils of the Scottish Highlands. There are now over 900 000 hectares of land under trees in Scotland alone, well over half of which have been planted and are managed by the Forestry Commission — the rest being privately owned.

Afforestation (the growing of trees) takes place in a series of stages:

1. Ploughing. As much of the land owned by the Forestry Commission is peaty moorland ploughing takes place up and down the hillside. This cultivates the soil and the furrows allow the surface water to drain away easily and provide a place for the planting of young trees.
2. Growing of young trees in nurseries. Seeds (taken from cones dried in an oven) are sown in **nurseries** where the soil is sandy and has few weeds. They are looked after for three to four years until they are hardy enough for the hillside.
3. Transplanting in forest. When ready the young trees are transported from the nursery and planted (usually by hand) in the turf turned up by the ploughs on the hillside.
4. Caring for trees in forest. Over the next few years the trees are carefully tended — by spraying with fertilizers and weed killers, often by helicopter.
5. Thinning. Twenty years later the poorer trees are thinned out (about 50%) by chainsaw to allow more light to reach the best trees and to allow the trunks to thicken. Every 5 years the trees are thinned a bit more. These young trees are sold as 'standing timber' e.g. for poles, fencing and making pulp (for paper).

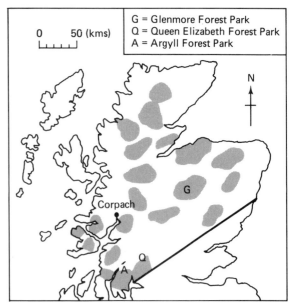

Fig. 203   The main forested areas in the Highlands

6. Clearfelling. Fifty years after planting the remaining crop is harvested. Trees are felled by chainsaw (the branches being cut off and left to rot with the stumps) then specially adapted machinery transports the trees to the forest edge.
7. Removal. Once at the roadside the timber is cut into convenient lengths and stacked for collection. The large logs go for saw milling, building timber and pallet making. The smaller ones go to make pulp, hardboard or particle board. The next year the ground is prepared for replanting and the whole process starts again.

The original trees planted by the Forestry Commission after the First World War have reached maturity and so output of timber is now very high.

Conservation
In the past many of the forests planted were criticised as being dark, artificial and ugly blobs on the hillsides. Today however much has been done to change this. The diagram Fig. 204 shows that a much greater variety of species have been planted, many now being of the natural 'broadleaved' type e.g. beech and

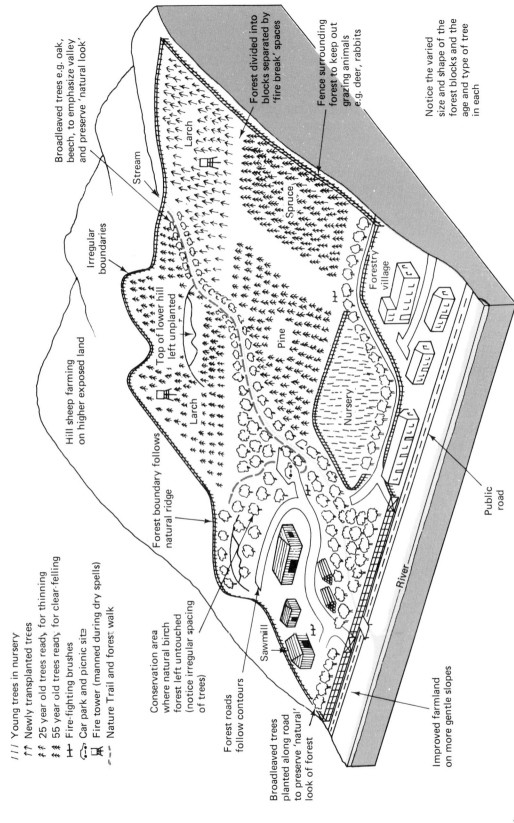

/ / / Young trees in nursery
↑↑ Newly transplanted trees
⚶⚶ 25 year old trees ready for thinning
⚶⚶ 55 year old trees ready for clear-felling
⊣⊢ Fire-fighting brushes
🏠 Car park and picnic site
🏯 Fire tower (manned during dry spells)
⚊⚊ Nature Trail and forest walk

Broadleaved trees e.g. oak, beech, to emphasize valley and preserve 'natural look'

Forest divided into blocks separated by 'fire break' spaces

Fence surrounding forest to keep out grazing animals e.g. deer, rabbits

Notice the varied size and shape of the forest blocks and the age and type of tree in each

Stream

Larch

Spruce

Irregular boundaries

Hill sheep farming on higher exposed land

Top of lower hill left unplanted

Pine

Forestry village

Larch

Nursery

Forest boundary follows natural ridge

Public road

Conservation area where natural birch forest left untouched (notice irregular spacing of trees)

Forest roads follow contours

Sawmill

River

Broadleaved trees planted along road to preserve 'natural' look of forest

Improved farmland on more gentle slopes

Fig. 204   Typical forested area in the Highlands

145

oak, especially along the roads passing through the forests and along nature trails. The regimented rows which used to exist have now been altered to blend with the contours and prominent landmarks like crags, streams and waterfalls are no longer hidden so that the forest has a much more 'natural' look. In addition forests are the home of many types of wildlife. The Commission recognises this and so does all it can to safeguard and improve the woodlands as wildlife habitats and gives particular attention to those areas where nature conservation has been identified as being of special importance.

Recreation

The Commission also realises the important part forests can play in providing recreation for the general public and so several 'Forest Parks' e.g. Glenmore Forest Park, have been opened to the public where facilities like car parks, picnic places, viewpoints, forest walks, nature trails, caravan sites, camping sites and information centres have been provided. In return the public are asked to follow the 'Country Code' – in particular to take great care to ensure that no fires are started (since this is of course the greatest danger to the well-being of a forest) to keep to the trails and pathways set out and ensure all litter is dropped in baskets provided.

Exercise

1 Give the reasons for the formation of the Forestry Commission in 1919. *2 marks*

2 Examine the model of a typical forested area in the Highlands (Fig. 204) and
    (a) Describe four attempts made to give this forest a more 'natural look'. *4 marks*
    (b) Name the major natural threat to such a forested area. *1 mark*
    (c) Describe two features shown on the model designed to reduce this threat. *1 mark*

3 Describe and write explanatory notes on the photographs, Figs. 205 and 206. *4 marks*

4 Explain what is meant by (a) thinning (b) clearfelling in forestry. *2 marks*

Fig. 205

Fig. 206

5 Examine the area enclosed by Glenmore Forest Park on O.S. Map 9.
    (a) Explain what is meant by a Forest Park. Illustrate your answer using at least three features from the map (give six-figure grid references). *4 marks*

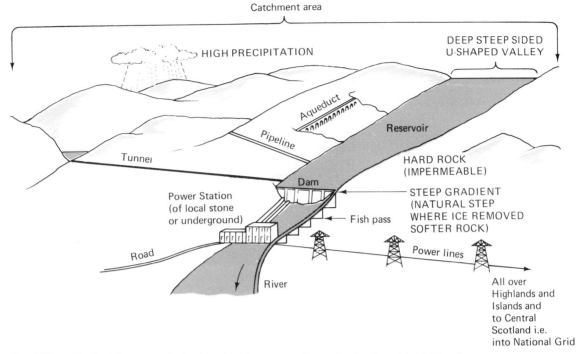

Fig. 207 Typical features of a hydro-electric power scheme in the Scottish Highlands

(b) How is the park boundary represented on this map? *1 mark*

(c) Examine square 9711 in which the forest fence runs from NW to SE.

(i) Explain the need for such a fence. *½ mark*

(ii) Suggest why the land to the north east of this fence is not forested. *½ mark*

Total 20 marks

Hydroelectric power in the Highlands

Hydroelectric power (H.E.P.) is produced using the action of running water (see Fig. 177 on p. 125). This method of producing power makes an important contribution to energy supplies, where little pollution results, and the raw material (water) can be used over and over again i.e. it is a **renewable** source of power, unlike coal or oil which can be used only once. Most H.E.P. in Scotland is produced in the western and central Highlands. Fig. 207 shows the main advantages this area has for the development of H.E.P. Stations.

Exercise

Examine the sketch Fig. 207 and answer the following questions:

(a) Explain in your own words how electricity is produced in an H.E.P. scheme. Refer to Fig. 177 on page 125 to help you. Use the words generator, reservoir, dam, power-station and turbine.

(b) The words written in capital letters are **five** of the advantages the Highland landscape has for the production of H.E.P. Copy and complete the table Fig. 208 explaining why each advantage encourages the development of an H.E.P. scheme.

(c) What do you think the term **catchment area** means?

(d) Write down three ways in which the catchment area of the H.E.P. scheme shown in Fig. 207 has been increased in size.

The North of Scotland Hydroelectric Board

The first people to make use of the Highlands' advantages for H.E.P. production were the British Aluminium Company. They built Britain's first large-scale H.E.P. station in 1894 at Foyers (see Fig. 178 on p. 126) to

Characteristic	Why is this an advantage?
Hard rock	
Impermeable rock	
High precipitation	
Deep valley	
Natural 'steps' on valley floors	

Fig. 208

provide the large amounts of power needed to smelt aluminium at their nearby aluminium works. There were however few other developments until 1943 when the **North of Scotland Hydroelectric Board** (NSHEB) was set up to provide electricity for this remote part of the U.K. These aims have been largely successful since the development of H.E.P. has brought several improvements to the Highlands:

1. Electricity has been provided for 99% of the people living in the Highlands even in the remote valleys and islands — (supplied through submarine cables);

2. The construction, maintenance and control of H.E.P. schemes provides jobs for local people;

3. Because of the improvement in power supply and encouragement from the NSHEB many new industries have been attracted to the Highlands providing even more jobs;

4. New roads have been built up to the dams and so many areas are much less isolated than they used to be;

5. Farming techniques have been improved, e.g. crofts are less dependent on dry weather since grains can be dried indoors using electric fans;

6. The construction of dams helps reduce flooding and river erosion downstream.

Conservation of the Highland environment

In the early years many people were opposed to the construction of hydroelectric schemes. The main complaints were:

(a) The scenery would be spoiled by large dams, aqueducts, pipelines, power stations and electricity pylons stretching across the countryside;

(b) Building a reservoir meant flooding a river valley or raising the level of a loch so many plants and smaller creatures would be destroyed and the spawning grounds of salmon would be flooded;

(c) The dams would prevent migrating fish like salmon and sea trout from moving up and down the river and so the fish population would drop.

In recent years however the NSHEB have managed to convince most people that these fears are unfounded. To do this they have taken several important steps. Several power stations have been built underground out of sight; others have had their outer walls covered by local stone so that they blend in with the scenery, while others have been hidden amongst trees. Power cables follow valleys where they are least conspicuous and avoid areas where the scenery is particularly valuable.

Special measures have also been taken to protect fish e.g. fish ladders (or the new 'fish lifts') have been built at most reservoirs so that the dam no longer provides an obstacle to the migrating fish. A 'fish lift' works in a

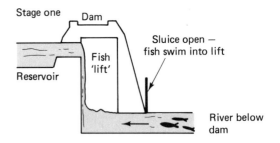

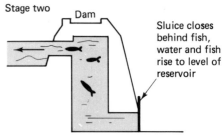

Fig. 209 How a 'fish lift' works

similar way to a lock on a canal (see Fig. 209). The fish can by-pass the dam in a series of steps with little or no effort.

In the reservoirs where the spawning grounds have been flooded, traps have been set to catch salmon. The fish are then stripped of their eggs. The eggs are then reared in hatcheries and set free in a suitable river.

Other measures taken to protect fish numbers include the building of protective screens round the dams so that the fish are not damaged, and the removal of steep waterfalls so that the fish can reach the spawning grounds more easily.

Finally, some would say that far from spoiling the landscape, the H.E.P. schemes are among the most impressive sights to be seen in the Highlands and that they **add** to the beauty of the Highland scenery.

Pumped storage schemes
The main power stations in Britain are now linked together by a **national grid** so that if power is in short supply in one part of the country it can be transported from areas where there is a surplus. The advantage of H.E.P. stations is that they can be turned on and off in minutes to meet sudden changes in demand.

Two of the most important H.E.P. schemes are Cruachan on Loch Awe (Fig. 211) and Foyers on Loch Ness (see Fig. 178 p. 126). Both are pumped storage schemes.

A **pumped storage scheme** is a hydroelectric scheme where the turbines can turn both ways and so as well as generating electricity they can pump water back into the storage reservoir using energy from the national grid.

The Cruachan pumped storage scheme

The Cruachan H.E.P. station, part of the Loch Awe hydroelectric scheme is the largest of the two pumped storage stations in Scotland. The main features of this development are shown on the sketch Fig. 210: notice the small high level dam (400 m above sea level) and the cavern (Fig. 213) cut deep into the mountainside containing the power station.

At various times in the day the demand for electricity is very high i.e. at 'peak' periods. At such times the sluice gates on the storage dam are opened (see diagram), the water rushes down to the turbines, rotating them. This in turn drives a generator producing electricity which is then transmitted by cable to a transformer and on to the national grid. The water leaving the turbines is slowed down in the surge chamber then flows through the **tailrace tunnel** into Loch Awe.

During '**off peak**' periods (especially at night and weekends) the surplus energy produced by power stations in other parts of Scotland is transmitted to Cruachan where it turns the turbines in the opposite direction.

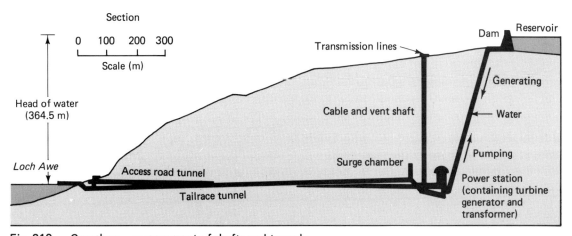

Fig. 210   Cruachan — arrangement of shafts and tunnels

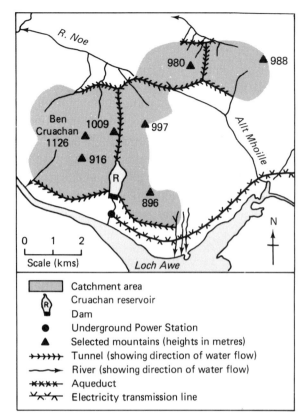

Fig. 211   The Cruachan pumped storage scheme

Fig. 213

Exercise

1 What benefits has the development of H.E.P. brought to the Highlands?

2 Unlike anglers in the past few now object to H.E.P. schemes being developed in the lochs where they fish. Give at least four reasons for this change in attitude.

3 Describe some of the measures taken by the NSHEB to ensure that the natural scenery of the Highlands has not been ruined by H.E.P. developments.

4 Write down the meaning of the following words: **Aqueduct, Peak period, Pumped storage scheme, Tailrace tunnel.**

5 Examine Fig. 211 and Fig. 212 showing the Cruachan Pumped Storage Scheme.
   (a) During the night water flows up to the reservoir. Explain how and why this happens.
   (b) Where does the energy for this process come from?
   (c) 'The Head of water' of an H.E.P. scheme is the height through which the water falls from the top of the dam onto the power station. Using Fig. 210 state the 'Head of water' at Cruachan Dam.
   (d) Explain why a large 'Head of water' is necessary to an H.E.P. scheme.

Fig. 212   Cruachan dam

The turbines thus act as pumps forcing water from Loch Awe back up to the storage reservoir on Ben Cruachan. In this way the energy is stored high up in the reservoir ready for the next 'peak period'. A pumped storage scheme therefore acts in a similar way to a battery i.e. it stores energy.

The growth of tourism in the Highlands

One industry which is continually growing, not only in the Highlands but in most parts of th world is **tourism**. Each year thousands of tourists flock into the Highlands from home and abroad, to take advantage of the beautiful scenery, the peace and quiet, the hills and mountains for walking and climbing, the rivers and lochs for angling and the different plant and animal wildlife all of which are extremely attractive features to people used to living in large towns and cities.

Since the 1950s the number of tourists visiting the Highlands has increased remarkably — largely because people have more money to spend, longer holidays with pay and many more have their own car i.e. people have become richer and more mobile. As a result tourism has become one of the Highlands 'growth' industries, bringing millions of pounds a year into the area. In an effort to encourage this growth many steps have been taken. New indoor facilities e.g. leisure centres and amusement arcades have been provided in some resorts to provide 'rainy weather' entertainment. New roads have been built, while others have been straightened and widened. More ferries (including car ferries) have been laid on to the islands, special cheap rail tickets have been introduced and the number of coach tours has increased. New tourist information

centres and picnic, camping and caravan sites have also been created. New hotels and shops have sprung up, while others have expanded and many farmhouses and crofts have been converted into bed and breakfast accommodation. Finally, the amount of publicity advertisements on T.V. and in the form of holiday brochures, has increased greatly in order to attract peoples' attention to the area and encourage them to visit.

Employment
The influx of tourists has had a great effect on the local Highland people. Thousands of **jobs** have been created e.g. in hotels, restaurants, cafes, bars, garages and in the craft industries (which produce thousands of souvenirs e.g. tartan clothing, perfume and ornaments).

A major problem with this type of employment however is that it is generally **seasonal**. Many more people visit the Highlands in the **summer** and so many towns and villages which are teeming with people in summer are almost empty in winter. There are

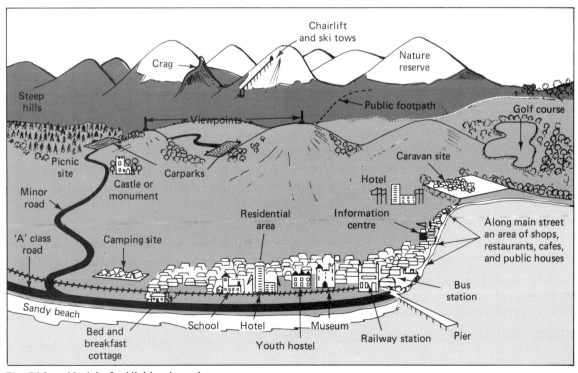

Fig. 214   Model of a Highland tourist resort

151

therefore fewer jobs available in the winter in these resorts. This has become less of a problem in some places however with the development of winter sports and the construction of indoor facilities e.g. Aviemore (see p. 161).

Model of a Highland resort
Fig. 214 shows some of the features found in many Highland tourist resorts. These features encourage **active recreation** (where people involve themselves in strenuous activity e.g. skiing, hillwalking, sailing) and **passive recreation** (where people relax and enjoy the scenery e.g. picknicking, walking along a beach, sunbathing).
Note: buildings or small sites where people can enjoy their leisure time e.g. picnic sites, are often referred to as **recreational nodes,** while larger areas, e.g. sandy beaches are referred to as **recreational zones.** A recreational zone often contains several recreational nodes.

Exercises

1 Explain why the **tourist industry** has become a 'growth industry' in many parts of the world in the last thirty years.

2 Describe some of the attractions of the Scottish Highlands for the tourist.

3 Describe some of the steps taken to encourage the growth of tourism in the area.

4 Explain what is meant by 'seasonal employment'.

5 O.S. Map 8.
Examine the area around Kyle of Lochalsh enclosed by the squares shown in Fig. 215.
(a) Give two pieces of map evidence which suggest that there is a **passive recreation zone** in square 7727. Explain your answer for each.
(b) Give one piece of map evidence which suggests that square 8228 is an **active recreation zone.** Explain your answer.
(c) Identify one **active recreation node** in square 7527. Explain your answer.
(d) Using the map copy and complete the following table (Fig. 216) listing as many similarities and differences as you can.

A comparison between a model Highland resort (Fig. 214) and Kyle of Lochalsh	
Similarities	Differences
Both have bed and breakfast accommodation	
Both have an area of shops, restaurants, public houses, etc., along main street	

Fig. 216

(e) Explain the importance of the 'A' class road and the railway line to the tourist industry in Kyle of Lochalsh.

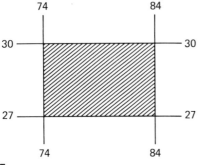

Fig. 215

152

9
The Highland problem (depopulation) and the Growth Areas

Exercise

Study the graph, Fig. 217. Describe the changes since 1851 in:

(a) The total population of the Orkney Islands;
(b) The population of Kirkwall;
(c) The population of the Island of Shapinsay.

Similar trends have been experienced in most other parts of the Highlands. A small number of towns have grown as ports, service centres or small scale industrial centres but that growth has been very slow and the Highlands has remained a generally rural area. Even today there are only five towns with over 10 000 inhabitants — all are in the eastern lowlands.

For over 200 years (up until the 1960s) the Highlands was an area of **depopulation** i.e. the population decreased as more people left the area than came into it.

Why were people leaving the Highlands?

Depopulation began in the 18th century when thousands of highlanders were forcibly evicted from their homes by their landlords to make way for sheep farmers from the south who could afford to pay higher rents for the land. Some moved to small areas of land around the coast but many emigrated to the 'new' countries of North America and Australia.

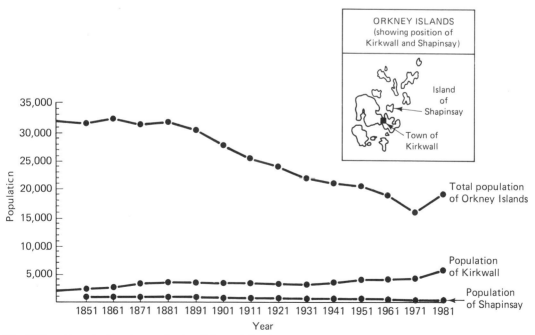

Fig. 217   Population change in the Orkney Islands

This drift away from the Highlands continued right through to the middle of this century. Increased mechanisation meant less work for people on farms and crofts, while the lack of raw materials, poor communications and isolation from large markets made the area unattractive to most types of industry so unemployment was, until recently, much higher in the Highlands than elsewhere in the country.

Even for those with jobs life can be extremely tough in the Highlands e.g. the harsh physical environment (see Fig. 197) ensures that crofters must work very hard for little financial reward. From lower incomes they must pay more for almost everything they buy since most goods must be transported long distances from where they are produced. Furthermore large areas of the Highlands suffer from a shortage of amenities like cinemas, discos, shops and sport facilities, and some townships have only recently been supplied with electricity and piped water. (Mobile amenities like travelling shops, banks and film shows make their way regularly around many of the crofting townships.) Although the standard of education is high, schools in some areas are few and far between (many only have one teacher). Young children often have to walk or be driven several kilometres each day, often in bad weather, in order to get to school, while many older pupils live away from home in secondary boarding schools.

Once young people have tasted the 'bright lights' of the towns they often decide to leave the rural areas altogether and look for work and an easier more varied life in towns either within the Highlands or elsewhere in the country.

As a result of such depopulation many communities (particularly those in the western Highlands and islands) are now populated mainly by older people and there is a real danger that some of these communities could die out altogether before too long.

Exercise

1 The two diagrams in Fig. 218 are called **population pyramids**. A population pyramid describes the **structure** of a place's population i.e. it shows the sex and ages of the people living there. There are two scales on a population pyramid. Five year age groups are marked on the vertical scale, and the percentage of the total population in these age groups is marked on the horizontal scale. The pyramid is divided into two halves with the females on the right and males on the left. By examining the horizontal bars it is possible to find out the percentage of the total population in each age group e.g. in Inverness 4% of the total population are males between the ages of 10 and 14. Examine these two pyramids and answer questions (a)–(d).

    (a) What percentage of the total population is between the ages of 15 and 39 in (i) Inverness and (ii) Harris?

    (b) What percentage of the total population is 75 or over in (i) Inverness and (ii) Harris?

    (c) Explain in at least 30 of your own words your answer to questions (a) and (b).

    (d) This 'top heaviness' of Harris's population structure is increased by retired people from the towns coming to live there. Why do you think these people are attracted to such rural areas?

2 In the background of Fig. 199 a sight common throughout the Highlands can be seen. Describe what the photograph shows and suggest an explanation for your answer.

3 Imagine your family lived on a croft on the island of Lewis, that you went to Secondary School in Stornoway, then went to college in Glasgow until you were 21.

    (a) List as many reasons as you can why you might then want to return to your family's crofting township to live.

    (b) Make a second list — this time of reasons why you might **not** want to return there but stay in Central Scotland.

    (c) State whether you would eventually decide to return home to live or stay in Central Scotland.

Unfortunately for the crofting areas, most young people decide **not** to return there to live.

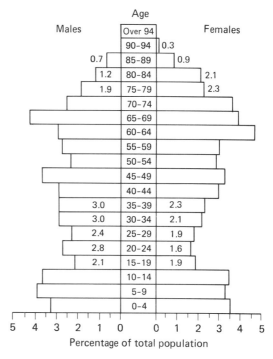

Fig. 218   Population pyramids for an urban and a rural area in the Highlands

(Notice that actual percentage figures are inserted for same age groups)

4 (a) Examine a map of the United States or Canada and make a list of Scottish surnames or names of Scottish places shown (e.g. can you find any 'Macs'?).
(b) Try to explain why these names are used so far from Scotland.

5 O.S. Map 8.
(a) Study the O.S. map carefully then describe and explain the distribution of the settlements shown on it. (Your explanation should refer to the relief and drainage of the area.)
(b) Using two of the three words below complete the following sentence: nucleated; dispersed; linear. 'The arrangement of buildings in Arnisdale (square 8410) could be described as _____ while those in Kylerhea (square 7820) are much more _____ .
(c) Explain this difference in your own words.
(d) Examine the village of Isleornsay (square 7012) and write down **five** sources of employment which may be available to local crofters.
(e) Can you see any evidence of population decline on the part of the Isle of Skye shown on this map?
(f) Explain why food prices in Isleornsay are likely to be slightly higher than those in Dornie (square 8826).

6 Examine the **Amenity Index table** Fig. 219 and the **scatter graph** Fig. 220.
Along the top of Fig. 219 are the names of five settlements in the area covered by the O.S. map. Down the left-hand side are a series of amenities, each with an index number. The higher the index number the more important the amenity to the settlement. For example, a railway station (index No. 4) is more important than a telephone box (index No. 1). Along the bottom of the table is the approximate number of houses (a rough measure of settlement size) in each settlement.
(a) Using your O.S. map, copy and complete the Amenity Index table (e.g. Kyle of Lochalsh is on three ferry routes (index No. 3) so it is given 3 x 3 = 9 points in the table. Remember to calculate the total Amenity Index for all five settlements.
Using the Amenity Index totals and numbers of houses it is possible to make up a **scatter graph** to see if there is any **correlation** or relationship between the number of amenities and the number of houses in

Index number	Amenity	Kyle of Lochalsh (square 7627)	Dornie (sq. 8826)	Glenelg (sq. 8119)	Kyleakin (sq. 7526)	Kirton (sq. 8327)
3	On ferry route	9	0	0	3	0
4	Railway station	□	0	0	0	0
3	On 'A' class road	3	3	0	3	3
1	On other road	1	1	2	0	0
1	Pier	3	0	0	1	0
2	Post office	2	2	0	□	0
1	Telephone	0	0	0	0	□
2	School	2	0	□	0	0
2	Church	6	2	4	□	2
2	Hotel	2	0	0	2	0
1	Youth hostel	□	0	0	0	0
3	Bridge over loch	0	3	0	0	0
1	Information centre	□	0	0	0	0
AMENITY INDEX TOTAL		□	11	□	□	□
Approximate no. of houses		170	45	62	70	14

Fig. 219   Amenity Index table of selected settlements

these settlements. The scatter graph Fig. 220 shows the Amenity Index totals along the bottom and the number of houses up the left-hand side. Each settlement can therefore be marked (or plotted) on the scatter graph.

(b) Copy the scatter graph and mark on the position of the settlements. Dornie has already been plotted.

(c) Four of the settlements should lie within the dotted area on the scatter graph. This allows a 'best fit line' to be drawn i.e. a line which indicates the general relationship between the Amenity Index totals and the number of houses. Draw in the best fit line.

(d) Only one sentence from the following three correctly describes the correlation between the amenities and number of houses in these settlements. Write the correct one in your jotter.

The number of amenities is equal to the number of houses.

The greater the Amenity Index, the greater the number of houses.

The greater the Amenity Index, the fewer the houses.

(e) As it stands this scatter graph is only of limited value in illustrating this relationship. How could it be made more accurate?

(f) Which of the five settlements does not come near the best fit line?

(g) Can you suggest a reason why this settlement differs from the others.

(h) Suggest another way of measuring the size of a settlement, other than by the number of houses.

The Highlands and Islands Development Board

Although various attempts had previously been made to reverse the process, depopulation of the Highlands continued into the 1960s (see Fig. 221).

The government of the time therefore decided that new stronger measures were necessary and so in 1965 a special board called **The Highlands and Islands Development Board** (HIDB) was set up. Its headquarters are in Inverness and it has powers to encourage development, in the area shown in Fig. 222, in an attempt to attract people back there to live.

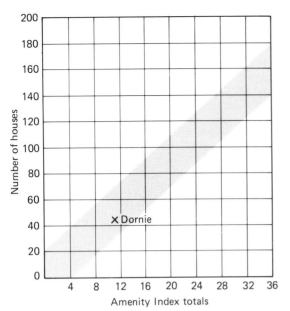

Fig. 220   Scatter graph showing correlation between amenities and number of houses

What can the HIDB do to help?
The HIDB operates in three main ways;
1. Most of its work and money goes into providing favourable **loans** or **grants** to developers wishing to start or expand a business in the area.
2. The board also carries out **projects of its own** e.g. in some areas it builds factories in advance to encourage industry to move there. It also tries to create development in more remote areas (where the risk of failure is too great for most businessmen) by carrying out projects like the construction of hotels and fish-processing facilities in the Outer Hebrides.
3. The board gives **advice** to businessmen, local authorities and the government on individual projects and broader issues. It also carries out **research** and **surveys** into the problems of the Highlands as well as **publicity campaigns** to attract industry into the area.

There are four working divisions within the HIDB.

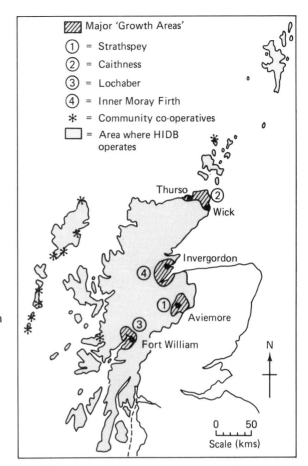

Fig. 222   Area of responsibility of the HIDB

1. The Land Development Division helps with the development of agricultural projects e.g. improving livestock and machinery. It also tries to find new markets for products and provides support for crofters.
2. The Fisheries Development Division helps provide boats, fish-processing facilities and fish farms.
3. The Industrial Development Division provides help for manufacturing industries. Three main 'Growth Areas' have been identified and promoted as particularly suitable for large scale industry since they

Year	1921	1931	1951	1961	1971	1981
Population	371,372	323,277	316, 471	304,161	307,103	352, 572

(Western Highlands = area shown in Fig. 222)

Fig. 221   Population change in the Western Highlands

157

have advantages like good transport facilities, flat land and a large available labour supply. These areas are in Caithness, Lochaber and around the Inner Moray Firth (see Fig. 222).

Smaller businesses have been encouraged throughout the HIDB area including those in the traditional industries like whisky distilling and 'newer' industries like the craft industry and electronics.

Although many of these small businesses only employ a very small number of people (some have less than 10 workers!) they are of vital importance in encouraging people to live in rural communities.

4. The Tourist Development Division tries to increase the quantity and quality of catering and tourist accommodation throughout the Highlands. The Strathspey area (see Fig. 222) has been promoted as a major tourist **Growth Area** in a similar way to the industrial growth areas mentioned above.

Note:

1. The HIDB not only provides help for profit-making (**commercial**) projects but also for **social** projects e.g. improving village amenities like halls, community centres, and various clubs.

2. Several parts of the Highlands e.g. Western Isles are too remote and have too few people for them to attract many businessmen. As a result the HIDB has encouraged the development of **community cooperatives** (see Fig. 222) in such areas. In these cooperatives local people are encouraged to get together and provide money for projects which would be for the good of the whole community e.g. social projects like building piers, and village halls or commercial projects like building holiday chalets, snack bars and market gardens. Although the HIDB provides half of the cost of these developments the projects are controlled by the people of the community i.e. the HIDB is helping them to help themselves.

Exercise

1 The Highlands of Scotland encompass the area north of the Highland Boundary Fault. Fig. 222

shows that the HIDB only operates in the western two-thirds of this area. Try to explain why.

2 Examine the following note carefully, then answer the questions below: In our study of industry in Central Scotland we learned that we can classify industries into heavy or light industries depending on the type of product made. Another way of classifying industries apart from heavy or light is shown below.
Primary Industries — the workers extract raw materials from the earth or sea, e.g. farming, mining, fishing.
Secondary Industries — the workers make (manufacture) products from these raw materials, e.g. in a steel works, knitwear or paper mill.
Tertiary Industries — the workers serve the public e.g. by selling or distributing these manufactured products or selling their own experience and skills e.g. shopkeepers, lorry drivers, doctors.

Primary	Secondary	Tertiary

Fig. 223

(a) Copy and complete the table Fig. 223 by placing the following industries in the appropriate column: Whisky distilling, Coal mining, Teaching, Banking, Drilling for oil, Fishing, Fish processing, Shipbuilding, Lumbering.
(b) Add another two industries of your own to each column.
(c) Describe the information shown on Fig. 224.
(d) Explain how the HIDB can encourage development within the Highlands.

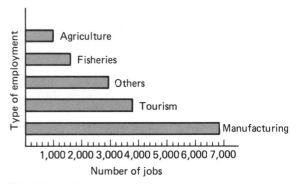

Fig. 224   Employment created with HIDB assistance 1972–1981

3 Dotted throughout the HIDB area are many examples of small-scale industries. Why does the HIDB consider these industries to be so important?

4 (a) Explain what is meant by a **community cooperative** in at least twenty of your own words.

(b) Examine the map, Fig. 222 and describe the distribution of these cooperatives.

(c) Explain why, even with HIDB help, relatively few outside businessmen are attracted into these areas.

Growth Area — Strathspey

The Strathspey Growth Area is shown in Fig. 225. In Strathspey the major development has been the growth of **tourist** and **recreational facilities**. This growth has been concentrated in the area around **Aviemore** one of the most important tourist centres in the Highlands, (shown in the photograph Fig. 226).

Exercise

O.S. Map 9

1 Examine Fig. 227 and with the aid of your O.S. map extract, name features A—E. Choose your answers from the following list: Cairngorm Mountains, Aviemore village, River Spey, Craigellachie (Hill), 'A' road and railway line.

2 'The natural characteristics of the landscape which have encouraged many generations of people to leave the Highlands have encouraged tourists into this area.'

(a) Explain this statement in at least 30 of your own words.

(b) List as many pieces of evidence as you can from the map which suggest that this area is regularly visited by tourists.

3 Using the map describe the **site** and **settlement pattern** of Aviemore in at least 20 of your own words.

The growth of tourism in and around Aviemore

Aviemore lies in the valley of the River Spey with the Cairngorm Mountains to the east and Monadhliath mountains to the west (these are two ranges forming part of the Highland plateau). Until the 1960s, Aviemore was just a small village on a railway junction with a few small hotels, visited by anglers, climbers and game hunters. As the tourist industry grew after the Second World War, Aviemore's

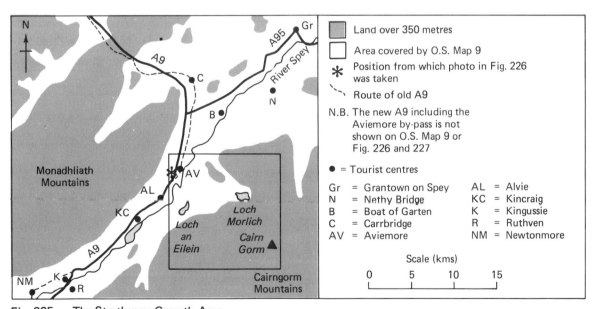

Fig. 225   The Strathspey Growth Area

159

Fig. 226   View of Aviemore from point 886121 — looking east-north-east

Fig. 227   Sketch of view shown in Fig. 226

Fig. 228   The Aviemore Centre

potential as a tourist centre was realised and the village began to grow slowly as a centre where tourists came for their summer holidays. In the 1960s this slow rate of growth was speeded up greatly mainly as a result of two major developments:

1. The construction of **ski facilities** on the northwest slopes of Cairn Gorm. In 1961 skiing became very popular on Cairngorm when the access road, car park (989 061) and chair lift were completed, allowing skiers to reach the ski-runs on Coire Cas (9904) and summer visitors to enjoy the hilltop scenery with much less effort. These facilities were improved in Coire Cas and extended into Coire na Ciste (square 0006) during the early 1970s.

Fig. 229   Curling in the Aviemore Centre

2. The development of **accommodation** particularly in or around the **Aviemore Centre** (893 124). As well as accommodation the centre provides many apres ski facilities which can be used all year round when it gets dark or when the weather makes outdoor activity unpleasant. New hotels, camping sites, caravan sites, a youth hostel and guest houses have since developed and the area shown on the map extract now provides overnight accommodation for around 6000 people i.e. almost half the tourist accommodation in the whole Spey valley.

All year round tourism
As a result of these developments people now visit Aviemore **all year round**, although as the graph, Fig. 231 shows, Aviemore is still at its busiest during the summer.

Nevertheless the winter tourist industry is vitally important. The ski facilities and the Aviemore Centre provide winter jobs for local people and so help solve the **seasonal unemployment** problem found in many other Scottish tourist resorts. In addition other industries related to tourism (in particular the craft industry) have also been encouraged in the area, creating further employment. The tourist industry has brought money into the area and the people now have amenities they never had before. As a result local people are encouraged to stay in Aviemore and outsiders have been encouraged to move in.

Although most local people have welcomed the developments of tourism and recreation there are some who have mixed-feelings about them e.g. they complain that they must now put up with higher prices in the shops, that many of the new jobs have gone to outsiders, and that the quiet way of life has been disturbed to a large extent by 'noisy tourists'.

Exercise

O.S. Map 9
1 Examine the graph Fig. 232:
    (a) Copy and complete table Fig. 233 by matching the decades to the appropriate description of population increase:
    Rapid increase, Moderate increase, Slight increase

So much to enjoy at Scotland's AVIEMORE Centre

Centre Caravan Park, Shops, Laundrette, Dry Cleaner	Ice Rink, Bar, Squash, Table Tennis, Coffee Shop, Games Room, Snooker
Loch Puladern, Fishing School, Nature Trail	Post House Hotel, Buttery
Putting Greens	A9 Perth — Inverness
Strathspey Hotel, Guddled Trout	Aviemore Chalets Motel, Craigellachie Bar
Children's Playground	Crazy Golf, Trampolines, Swing Ball
Helicopter Landing	Freedom Inn, Bank, Shops
AA Service Centre	British Rail, Strathspey Steam Railway
Deerstalker Bar, Beergarden	Kart Raceway
Osprey Room	District Heating Plant
Pinewood Restaurant	Staff Residence
Information Bureau	Conference and Marketing Office, Works Department
Fraser Room	Car Hire
Speyside Theatre, Cinema	Scotland's Clan Tartan Centre
Badenoch Hotel	Scandinavian Village
Dry Ski Slopes, Tow, Bike Hire, Fun Machines, Ski Bus Stop	Pony Trekking
Allander Square, Shops, Ski Hire, Games Room, Hairdressing	Highland Craft Village, Giant Chess
Swimming Pool, Sauna, Solarium, Shops, Post Box, Telephones	Santa Claus Land, Theme Rides, Gardens, Ginger Bread House
Das Stubel Restaurant	

Fig. 230

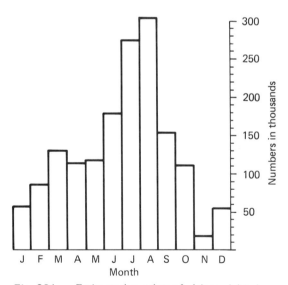

Fig. 231   Estimated number of visitor-nights in Strathspey in one year

(b) Explain the reasons for the increase in Aviemore's population since 1961 in at least 50 of your own words.

2 Examine the O.S. map and the sketch-map Fig. 234 and answer the following questions:

(a) Name the corries with existing ski facilities (A and B).

(b) Explain why the access road on your O.S. map (shaded yellow) is bounded by dashes (===) and not full lines (===).

(c) Explain the importance of 'Jeans Hut' (981 034).

(d) Explain the meaning of the symbol ✳ at 997 075.

(e) Explain why this symbol appears incomplete at point 988 062.

(f) The sketch-map shows two selected ski runs. Using your O.S. map explain why the slope represented thus − − − − is described as a 'difficult' ski run, while that represented thus . . . . . is described as an 'easy' run.

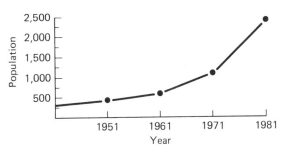

Fig. 232   Population increase in Aviemore 1951–81

3 Fig. 235 shows a simplified section in Coire na Ciste from **998 074** to **005 039**. If a skier wanted to reach the summit from the car park he/she would usually do so in four stages (A–D on the section).

(a) Describe the method of travel in each of the stages A–D shown on the section. (Choose from: footpath, 1st chairlift, 2nd chairlift, ski-tow).
(b) Through what **range** in altitude would a skier travel from the summit down to the car park?
(c) What would the average gradient of such a ski-run be?

4 Examine Fig. 236 and your O.S. map extract, and answer the following questions:

(a) The model area shows several features which may encourage ski-developments to take place there. Copy and complete the table Fig. 237 by:

(i) Explaining why each feature would be an advantage to ski-developments;
(ii) Deciding whether Coire Cas (9904) has each advantage or not.

(b) Suggest what effect a strong northerly wind would have on a day's skiing in the model corrie. Explain your answer.

(g) Grid reference **005 048** may seem a strange site for a restaurant. Nevertheless there is one at this point. Suggest two advantages this site has for such a restaurant in the mountains.

Decade	Population increase
1951–1961 1961–1971 1971–1981	

Fig. 233

Developed corries = A and B
Corries which could be developed = XY and Z
Restaurant = ■
'Jeans Hut' = O

Selected ski runs

— — — = Difficult
••••• = Easy

P⌐□ = Car park

Cairngorm National Nature Reserve

Steepest slopes

Access road

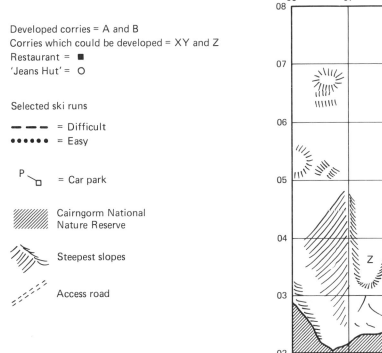
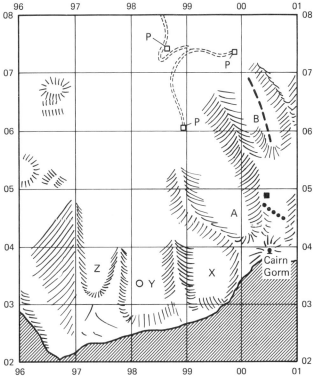

Fig. 234   Selected features on the Cairngorm slopes south-east of Aviemore

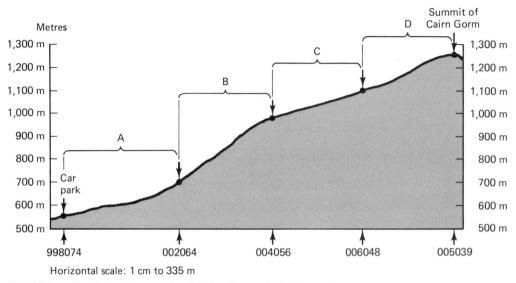

Fig. 235   Reaching the summit of Cairn Gorm via Coire na Ciste

5 Imagine visiting Aviemore on the three different occasions below:

    (i) A lovely summer's afternoon;

    (ii) A wet, windy summers day;

    (iii) A sunny calm winters day after a heavy fall of snow.

List the activities which could be enjoyed in each of these situations without leaving the area covered by the O.S. map.

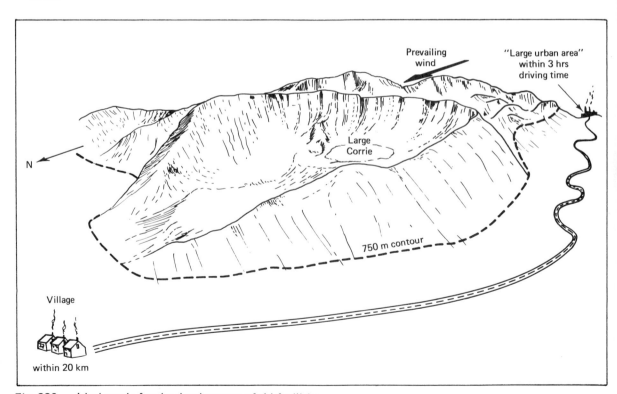

Fig. 236   Ideal corrie for the development of ski facilities

Features of ideal corrie	Why is this an advantage?	Does Coire Cas have this?
High back wall shelters corrie from prevailing wind		Yes
Corrie faces north		
Corrie lies above 750 m		
There is a large urban area within 3 hrs driving time		Yes
There is a small populated settlement within 20 kms		

Fig. 237

6 Examine Fig. 238. **Note:** the figures given are **not** actual numbers of tourists but the **percentage** of the tourist beds available which are occupied.

(a) Describe and try to explain the difference in the distribution of tourists throughout the year in the two resorts.

(b) Explain the smaller peak in occupancy rate in Aviemore in February and March.

(c) Name a west coast Highland resort.

(d) Which of the two resorts do you think would have the greater number of visitors over the year as a whole?

7 Aviemore and the other Speyside resorts, formerly lying on the A9 trunk road, have been by-passed as a result of road reconstruction and improvement.

(a) Suggest one reason why such by-passes are being built.

(b) Suggest what effect these road improvements may have on the Speyside tourist industry.

The Cairngorms land use conflicts

The attraction of so many visitors to the Highlands has caused two sets of problems in the area:

1. Conflicts among tourists e.g.:

(i) Game hunters complain that hill walkers scare deer at certain times of the year.

(ii) Tracks bulldozed to improve access to the hills for deer stalkers contribute to soil erosion and spoil the scenery for those who have come to appreciate it.

(iii) Game hunters illegally shoot birds of prey such as the golden eagle (Fig. 239) upsetting naturalists.

(iv) Retired people complain that they can no longer enjoy the peace and quiet that the small village of Aviemore used to provide, because of noise created by large numbers of incoming tourists.

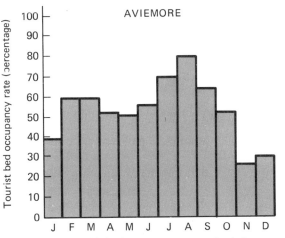
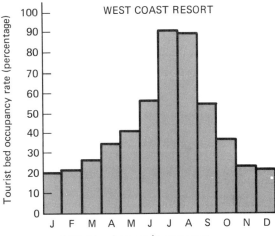

Fig. 238   Tourist bed occupancy rates in Aviemore and a west coast Highland resort in one year

Fig. 239   Golden Eagle

Fig. 240   Erosion in Glenmore Forest Park

2. Conservationists v developers

When thousands of people are attracted to an area like the Cairngorms, the scenery is inevitably changed. The tourists must have somewhere to sleep, they must be transported around the area and they must have facilities to amuse them in other ways. As a result new buildings, roads and other facilities are built, altering the environment greatly. Furthermore visitors seldom leave the area as they find it e.g. they leave litter lying around, they trample over vegetation, disturb wildlife and in many different ways spoil the beauty of the landscape. As a result many people called **conservationists** are opposed to developments which encourage large numbers of tourists into an area of such valuable scenery as the Cairngorms. Conservationists do all they can to see that an area's scenery is conserved i.e. remains unspoiled. They believe that the conservation of the scenery is much more important than any tourist development.

In an attempt to protect some of the Cairngorm scenery and wildlife much of the area has been designated as a National Nature Reserve, but even here the scenery and wildlife are not completely protected since the authorities have not yet been convinced that such protection is absolutely necessary for the good of the area and the country as a whole.

On many a winter's day the slopes of Coire Cas and Coire na Ciste are overcrowded with skiers, the car parks are jammed up by cars and buses and there are long queues for ski lifts and tows. There would therefore seem to be a demand for more ski facilities. With this in mind the Cairngorm Chairlift Company applied for permission to extend ski facilities into three other snowfields — Coire-an-t Sneachda (9903), Coire an Lochain (9803) and Lurcher's Gulley (9703) and to extend the access road up to them (see Fig. 234 on p. 163).

These plans were however opposed by conservationists, particularly the NCC (Nature Conservancy Council) and so before permission could be given a public inquiry (a meeting open to the public where interested people can argue 'for' or 'against' a development, to a committee who presents a report to the Secretary of State for Scotland) had to be held.

Fig. 241   Chairlifts on Cairn Gorm

Exercise

1 Examine the graph Fig. 242:
(a) Describe what it shows in your own words;
(b) Explain why the results shown are of concern.

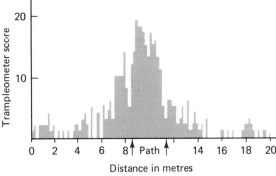

Fig. 242   Movement of walkers around a path on mountainside of Cairn Gorm

2 The photograph (Fig. 243) could well be used by conservationists to show how ski-development in the Cairngorms can affect the environment. Describe how the environment is affected in this photo.

3 Examine Fig. 234. X, Y and Z are corries which could be developed for skiing. Corrie Z is Lurcher's Gulley. Using O.S. Map 9 write down the names of corries X and Y.

4 A public inquiry in the classroom
Imagine that all the members of your class were present at the public inquiry meeting called to hear people's views on the proposed ski developments in the three corries mentioned above. Each pupil should play the part of one of the following people (or anyone else they think might attend such a meeting):
— Three committee members who will listen to everyone's views before sending a report to the Secretary of State.
— A wildlife expert who works for the NCC and who is concerned about the rare plants and animals living in the nearby nature reserve.

167

Fig. 243   Erosion on Cairn Gorm

— A representative from the Chairlift Company who argues that skiers usually keep to small areas of deep snow and that the Company are very skilled at re-seeding disturbed vegetation.
— An unemployed person living in Aviemore.
— A ski enthusiast.
— A pensioner living in Aviemore.
— An Aviemore housewife.
— An owner of a general store in Aviemore.
— A tourist who loves to come to Aviemore to admire the Cairngorm scenery.
— A rock climber and hillwalker who frequently visit these corries.
— A representative from the Scottish Tourist Board who wants to encourage foreign visitors to Scotland and so bring more money into the country (remember most visitors to Aviemore still come in summer).

Everyone should consider how the development would affect them, decide whether they are for or against them and present their argument as strongly as possible to the committee.

(a) After everyone has made their views clear to the committee each committee member should decide whether they would advise the Secretary of State to allow the developments to take place or not. Write down the committee decision in your jotter i.e. 3—0 for, 3—0 against, 2—1 for or 2—1 against.

(b) Which three arguments **for** the developments do you think were most convincing?

(c) Which three arguments **against** the developments do you think were most convincing?

(d) If you were the Secretary of State would you have allowed the developments to take place? Explain your answer.

In December 1982 the Secretary of State for Scotland decided that the developments should not take place i.e. that the conservationists argument was stronger than that of the developers.

Growth Area 2 — Caithness

The Caithness Growth Area is shown in Fig. 244. Here the major industrial development has been the **Nuclear Power Development Establishment,** employing over 2000 people at **Dounreay** 16 km west of the town of Thurso (Fig. 245). In 1954 the Atomic Energy Authority decided to construct an experimental 'fast' reactor power station. (Fast reactors allow much more energy to be obtained from a given amount of uranium than other types of reactor.)

The site at Dounreay was thought to be suitable for such a project for several reasons:-
1. Fast reactors were new, and to some extent unknown quantities and there was always the chance of radiation leaking out; therefore a remote location i.e. well away from cities and large towns, was thought to be necessary in case the area had to be evacuated;
2. There was a disused airfield built in a flat area of solid bedrock on which large heavy buildings could be built — there was even a disused camp of huts which provided accommodation for construction workers;
3. The government was keen to encourage development in the area in an attempt to halt the depopulation common throughout the Highlands;

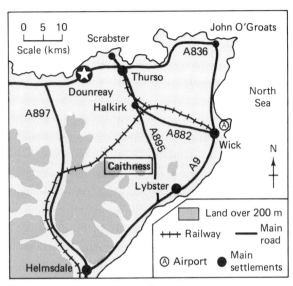

Fig. 244   The Caithness Growth Area

Fig. 245   Dounreay Nuclear Power Development Establishment

169

4. The coastal location provided water for cooling and producing steam and allowed easy transport of radioactive waste from the reactors.

The success of this reaction led in 1966 to a decision to build a second more powerful 'fast' reactor next to it. This second reactor (in the foreground of Fig, 245) has been producing electricity since 1974. The original reactor (rear right of photo) ceased production in 1977 but is now open as a public exhibition and museum of nuclear technology. Again the new reactor is mainly experimental – its fuel and components are studied continuously by scientists, engineers and economists from all over the world.

Impact on local community
The introduction of such a modern development to a remote part of Scotland had a huge effect on the local community. The establishment needed builders, scientists, engineers, technicians and office staff among other workers. As a result many locals left unemployed by the declining traditional industries found a job again, and so had less reason to leave the area. There were however too few people with appropriate training in the local area and so many **'atomics'** i.e. people highly trained in nuclear technology were imported from elsewhere in Scotland, the U.K. and abroad. Most of these were young, married couples who already had children, or were about to start a family and so the population structure became less 'top heavy'. These people brought fresh ideas and attitudes and so the whole area became revitalised and the trend towards depopulation reversed.

With the increase in population came the increased need for housing, roads, bridges, community centres, schools, banks and shops. The construction of such new services provided even more jobs, bringing more and more money into the community.

As the area became more prosperous new industries e.g. glass works, a plastic factory and a protective clothing factory were attracted and local farmers increased output to feed the larger population.

Education, not only for school children, but for school leavers and adults was improved greatly with the building of a technical college and the development of new training schemes for young adults – training them for work at Dounreay, and reducing their dependence on the declining traditional industries.

Exercise

1 Explain in your own words the need for the development of nuclear energy today.

2 What advantage does a fast reactor have over other nuclear power reactors?

3 (a) Suggest why the original Dounreay station was enclosed in a spherical cover (rear right of Fig. 245).
   (b) Now that there is no working reactor inside, state how the domed building is used today.

4 Explain in your own words why Dounreay was a good location for a nuclear power station.

5 Examine Figs. 244 and 245:
   (a) In which direction was the camera facing?
   (b) In which direction does Thurso lie?

Population of Caithness and Thurso			
	1951	1971	1981
Caithness	22,710	27,781	27,383
Thurso	3,249	9,087	8,828

Fig. 246

6 Examine Fig. 246 then describe and explain the changes in the population between 1951 and 1971 of:-
   (a) Caithness as a whole;
   (b) The town of Thurso.

7 Examine Fig. 247. Describe and explain the main changes in employment in Thurso between 1954 and 1966.

8 State three changes brought to Caithness as a result of the development of the Nuclear Energy Establishment at Dounreay other than those already mentioned in this exercise.

170

Type of employment	% of insured population		
	1954	1966	1978
Farming, fishing and forestry	24.0	7.0	6.9
Construction	21.0	8.8	10.2
Public administration	6.3	3.0	3.1
Food, drink and tobacco	4.7	1.0	0.4
Engineering	0.5	5.5	9.4
Scientific and technical	0	57.0	39.5

Fig. 247   Changes in employment structure in Thurso area 1954—78

Although Caithness has attracted a significant number of smaller scale industries in recent years these have not provided enough jobs for school leavers and those becoming unemployed from the traditional occupations like farming and fishing. Furthermore the Dounreay establishment has not significantly increased its workforce for a number of years.

As Fig. 246 shows one result of this situation has been that the population of the area has begun to decline again. The HIDB are therefore anxious that more development is attracted into Caithness in the future.

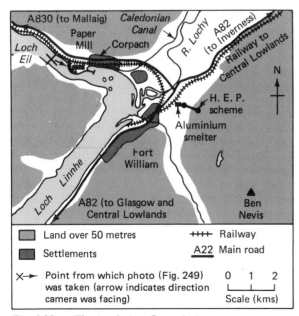

Fig. 248   The Lochaber Growth Area

Growth Area 3 — Lochaber

The Lochaber Growth Area, centered on **Fort William,** is shown in Fig. 248. Here the major industrial development has been the **pulp and paper mill** at Corpach which originally employed 900 people in converting local timber directly into paper. The nearby aluminium smelter is the second major employer in the area.

Why was a pulp and paper mill built at Corpach?

In 1966 the government loaned a company called Wiggins Teape two thirds of the £20 million needed to open the mill at Corpach in order to use the maturing timber resources of the Highlands and provide employment in the Fort William area. Find out why this site was chosen for the mill by completing the following exercise.

Exercise

1 Examine the sketch, Fig. 250, and name the features indicated by the letters A—H using Fig. 248 to help you.

2 Examine Fig. 250 and Fig. 203 (page 144) and list the reasons why Corpach was thought to be an excellent site for the development of a pulp and paper mill. (You should be able to list at least five reasons.) **Note:** the pulp and paper making process requires vast amounts of water.

3 One major disadvantage of the site has caused problems for the mill since it opened. What do you think this disadvantage is? (See Fig. 250.)

Impact on the community

The opening of the mill not only provided 900 jobs on the site but helped to employ 1500 workers in the surrounding forests (see p. 144). In Fort William itself new roads, houses, schools, shops and other amenities had to be built for the workers and their families so more employment was created.

The mill also saved the railway from closure since it was needed for transporting wood and paper. Had the mill not existed the

Fig. 249   An aerial view of the Fort William/Corpach area (looking east-south-east from point X on Fig. 248)

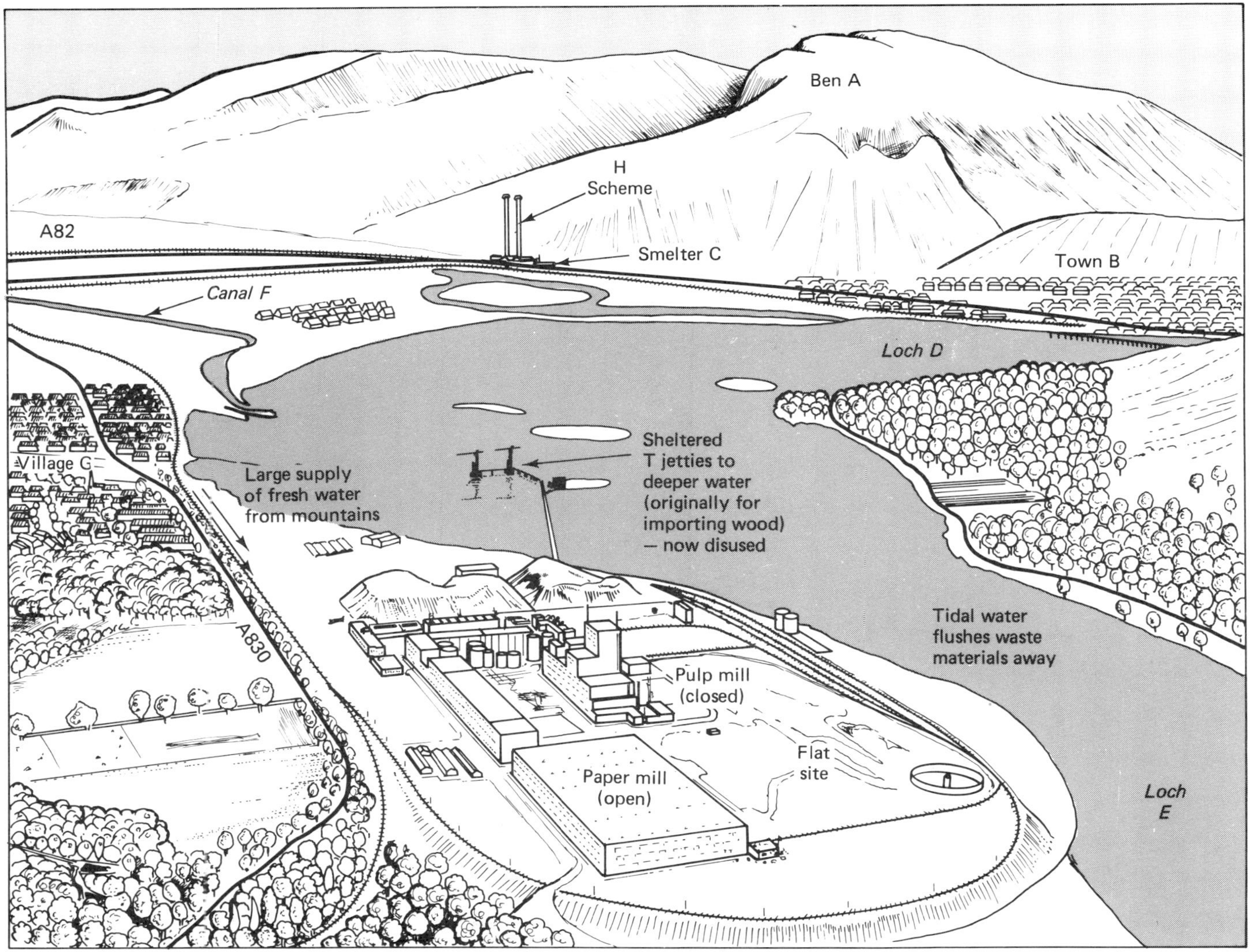

Ben A

Town B

Loch D

Loch E

A82

H Scheme

Smelter C

Sheltered
T jetties to
deeper water
(originally for
importing wood)
— now disused

Tidal water
flushes waste
materials away

Flat
site

Pulp mill
(closed)

Paper mill
(open)

Large supply
of fresh water
from mountains

Canal F

Village G

A830

Railways

A82   Main roads

Good communications for transporting materials
e.g. (originally) wood from nearby forests
(now) pulp from Scandinavia via Eastern ports
and paper out to markets (e.g. Central
Lowlands — 100 kms away)

Fig. 250   Sketch of Fig. 249

173

railway link to the Central Lowlands would have been closed down.

As a result of this increase in employment and numbers of amenities in Fort William, many people who had left the Highlands years before were attracted back again i.e. the trend towards depopulation was reversed in this area.

The closure of the pulp mill

This encouraging trend was however dealt a terrible blow. In 1980, 450 people lost their jobs when the pulp section of the mill was forced to close down as a result of high energy costs and competition from more efficient pulp mills in Scandinavia and Canada. The Highland timber is now transported to Scandinavia, made into pulp and returned to Corpach to be made into paper. Although this is an awkward process it does at least save the jobs of the workers in the Highland forests by providing a market for the timber.

Exercise

1 The Corpach mill was at one time the only integrated pulp and paper mill in the U.K.
   (a) Explain the meaning of 'an integrated mill'.
   (b) What advantage does an integrated mill have over separate pulp and paper mills?

2 List at least four ways in which the building of a pulp and paper mill was of benefit to the Fort William area.

3 (a) Highland timber is no longer sent to Corpach to be made into pulp. Explain why.
   (b) Where is the pulp for the Corpach paper mill made now?

Growth Area 4 — The Inner Moray Firth

Although **Inverness** is by far the largest settlement within this Growth Area, and is the main business, service and administrative centre in the whole HIDB area, the major industrial developments have taken place well to the north of the town's boundaries. In this Growth Area two major industries have developed.

The aluminium industry

In 1971 the British Aluminium Company built a large **smelter** at Invergordon (see Fig. 251). Its construction had similar beneficial effects to those resulting from the construction of a pulp and paper mill at Fort William i.e. it provided employment, brought money into the area and encouraged the growth of amenities like new roads, houses, shops and schools.

The closure of the smelter
Then just as at Fort William disaster struck when the smelter was closed down completely in 1981. Again high energy costs and competition from more efficient works elsewhere in the world were important reasons.
Conclusion
The story here then is very similar to that of the Fort William pulp mill — another large employer unable to survive in the Highlands. Work is already underway to try to encourage industrialists into the area at Fort William. Whether this will be successful or not or whether people will begin to drift away again and the area decline remains to be seen.

North Sea oil developments

Exercise

Examine O.S. Map 10
The development of North Sea oil has had a tremendous effect on industrial growth in this area. Several oil-related industries have grown up here in recent years. Fig. 251 shows their location and the number of people each employs. They have been drawn to the area not only by its natural physical attractions for such growth but by encouragement from the HIDB, the government, Highland Regional Council and the Cromarty Firth Port Authority.

1 What 'natural physical attractions' do you think the Inner Moray Firth area has for the development of oil-related industry? (See Figs. 136 and 251 and O.S. Map 10.)

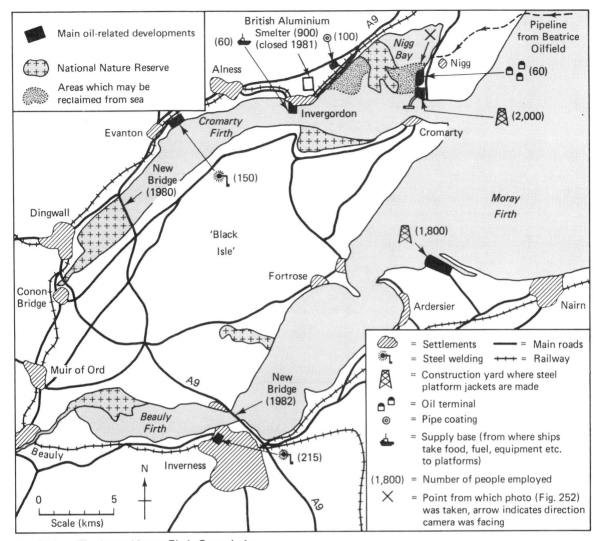

Fig. 251 The Inner Moray Firth Growth Area

2 Examine Figs. 251 and 252 and answer the following questions:

(a) Name the following features shown on Fig. 252 Bay A: Firth B, settlements C and D, North Sea oil developments E and F, road G, land use H.

(b) Feature J is not shown on the O.S. map. What does this suggest about the age of the photograph?

(c) Suggest the purpose of feature J.

(d) What map evidence is there that much of the land on which developments E and F are built has been reclaimed from the sea?

(e) From where does development F receive its main raw material?

(f) What is this 'raw material'?

(g) How is it transported to development F?

(h) Why is there no evidence of this method of transport on the photograph?

3 Fig. 253 shows a close up view of development E in Fig. 252. Write a short paragraph, of at least 50 words, to describe the industrial process carried out here. Use the following words in your description: **Nigg Bay, Steel platform, Dry dock, Floating raft, Oilfield, Jacket, 2000 jobs.**

4 The sand flats on Nigg Bay have been an important feeding ground for migrating birds for many years. Using map evidence describe one measure which has been taken to protect these feeding grounds against further industrial development.

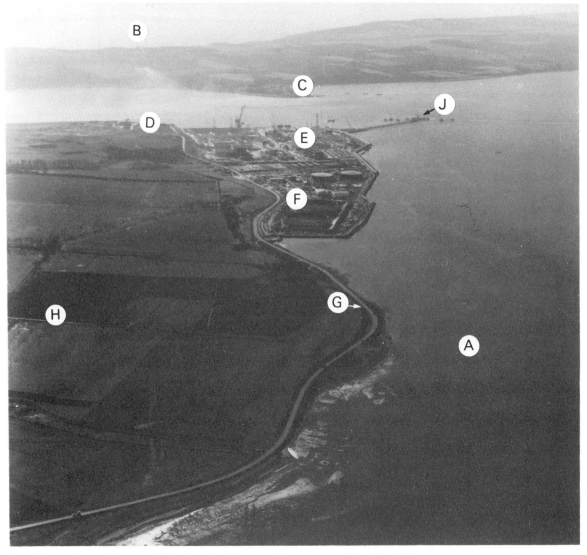

Fig. 252   An aerial view of Nigg Bay looking south from point X on Fig. 251

5   (a) How many new jobs have been created by the main oil-related developments in the Inner Moray Firth Growth Area? (See Fig. 251.)
    (b) One complaint among local people has been that too many of these jobs have gone to people from outside the area. Suggest why this has happened. (Think of the type of jobs involved.)
    (c) Another problem is that platform construction yards such as that at Ardersier often only provide 'cyclical employment'. Suggest what 'cyclical employment' might be and explain why the construction of platforms often only provides this type of employment.

6   (a) Look at Fig. 254 then copy and complete the bar chart using the population totals given in the table. (Invergordon has already been done for you.)
    (b) What does the graph reveal?
    (c) Try to explain these results.
    (d) What effect do you think the North Sea oil developments will have had on the depopulation of the Highlands?

Conclusion

An examination of the statistics in Figs. 217, 221 and 255 reveal that the trend towards depopulation has been reversed within many parts of the Highlands since the mid 1960s. The main factors contributing towards this change have been:-

Fig. 253

1. The introduction of large industrial employers like the Nuclear Power establishment at Dounreay, the mills at Corpach and the aluminium smelter at Invergordon.
2. (Probably the most important factor) – the work of the HIDB in encouraging developments in manufacturing, tourism, agriculture and fishing.
3. The discovery and development of North Sea oil and gas.
4. The work of other agencies like the NSHEB and the Crofters' Commission.

All these factors have helped provide or retain employment and improve living standards within the Highlands with the result that thousands of people have been encouraged into the area to live. Nevertheless various problems remain. The closure of the Corpach pulp mill and Invergordon aluminium smelter has meant a sharp rise in unemployment in these areas. Furthermore North Sea oil and gas will not last forever (recent estimates state that production levels will decline in the late 1980s). Finally the depopulation problem has returned to Caithness and continues in the more rural parts of the Highlands and the Western Isles (see Fig. 255).

The agencies mentioned above, particularly the HIDB must therefore continue to work at least as vigorously as they have done in the past if the success of the last twenty years is to be maintained or improved.

Exercise

Examine Fig. 255 and answer the following questions:

1 Describe the changes in population between 1971 and 1980 in (a) The Western Isles (b) Shetland.
2 marks

177

Population of Settlements

Settlement	1971	1981
Invergordon	2,350	4,050
Alness	2,560	6,248
Evanton	562	1,083
Dingwall	4,232	4,815
Muir of Ord	1,339	1,714

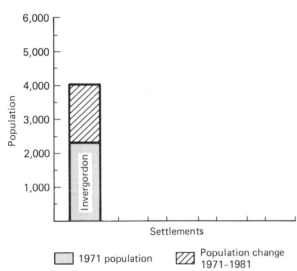

Fig. 254   Population change of settlements 1971–81

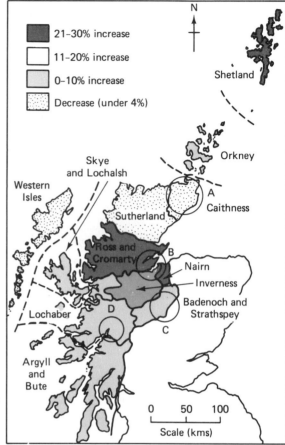

Fig. 255   % population change in HIDB area 1971–80 (by district or island area)

2 List some of the **reasons** for the change in population in (a) and (b) above. *5 marks*

3 **Crofting** is a way of life carried out by people living along the shores of the North West Highlands and on most of the islands shown on the map.

(a) List five characteristics of this way of life. *2½ marks*

(b) Name the organisation set up specifically to promote crofting in the Highlands. *½ mark*

(c) Describe one way in which the organisation helps solve some of the problems associated with crofting. *1 mark*

4 (a) Name the major industrial developments in each of the circles A–D, choose your answers from: **Paper mill, Nuclear power station, Tourist industry, Oil-related developments.** *2 marks*

(b) Choose one of these areas and write an account of the main development(s) found within it. You should mention the factors which attracted the developments; how successful they have been and the effects they have had on the local community. *7 marks*

Total 20 marks

Acknowledgements

The Publishers wish to thank the following
for their permission to use copyright
photographs and material:-

Cambridge University Collection of Air
   Photographs: pp. 5, 131b, 168;
Swiss Tourist Office: p. 7;
Farmers Weekly: p. 20;
Douglas Low: p. 21;
Scottish Farmer: pp. 22, 27, 141t;
Campbell Miller: pp. 29, 30, 31;
Hector Innes: pp. 38t, 44, 65;
Borders Regional Council: pp. 38b, 43t, 45;
John Dewar Studios: p. 39;
Scottish Woollen Industry, Edinburgh: p. 43b;
T & R Annan, Glasgow: p. 51;
Glasgow Herald: pp. 52, 54;
Norman Robertson: p. 53, 55, 57, 58t;
Strathclyde Passenger Transport Executive:
   p. 58b;
Scottish New Towns: pp. 61, 62;
National Coal Board: p. 71, 75;
South of Scotland Electricity Board: p. 73;
British Steel Corporation: pp. 79, 117t;
Aerofilms: pp. 81, 83, 112, 130, 131t, 140;
Honeywell Information Systems Ltd: p. 86;
British Petroleum: pp. 92, 93, 94b, 99, 101,
   116r;
Shell UK: p. 94t;
Technical Services Unit, City of Aberdeen:
   p. 96;

Clyde Port Authority: p. 104, 116l, 117b,
   119b;
Dundee College of Education: p. 119t;
Scottish Tourist Board: p. 134, 160, 161b;
Highlands & Islands Development Board:
   pp. 123, 138;
Skye Agencies: p. 141b;
Scotch Whisky Association: pp. 142, 143;
Forestry Commission: pp. 146, 166r;
North of Scotland Hydro-Electric Board:
   p. 150;
Jarrold & Son Ltd: p. 161t;
Natural History Photo Agency: p. 166l;
K M Andrew: p. 167;
United Kingdom Atomic Energy Authority:
   p. 169;
Wiggins Teape Group Ltd: p. 172;
Donald M Fisher: p. 176;
D G S Films Ltd: p. 177;
Ordnance Survey: p. 10;
British Rail: pp. 106, 107;
Geographical Magazine: pp. 162b, 167b;
Scottish Airports: p. 125t;
Scottish Development Agency: pp. 86r, 87;
Scottish Examination Board: p. 165b.
Cover photographs by courtesy of British
   Petroleum; Scottish Whisky Association
   and the Forestry Commission.